IRISH WRITERS
AND THEIR CREATIVE PROCESS

IRISH WRITERS
AND
THEIR CREATIVE PROCESS

edited by

Jacqueline Genet
and
Wynne Hellegouarc'h

IRISH LITERARY STUDIES 48

COLIN SMYTHE
Gerrards Cross, 1996

First published in Great Britain in 1996
by Colin Smythe Limited, Gerrards Cross, Buckinghamshire

British Library Cataloguing in Publication Data

A catalogue record for this book is available from the British Library

ISBN 0-86140-384-3

Distributed in the United States of America
by Oxford University Press Inc.
198 Madison Avenue, New York, NY 10016

Produced in Great Britain
Typeset by TuKan, High Wycombe
and printed and bound by T.J. Press (Padstow) Ltd., Cornwall

CONTENTS

To the memory of our dear friend

Gus Martin
1935–1995

INTRODUCTION

Jacqueline Genet

This volume contains the lectures delivered at Caen University in June 1992, for an international symposium organised by the Research Group in Anglo-Irish studies. The theme was the creative process, successively studied in three literary genres, poetry, drama and the novel. I had selected two of the most famous representatives in each genre, asking them to speak of their own creation. What happens in their minds during the birth and development of their creative work? A question which is far-reaching, abstruse and certainly indiscreet. To challenge the writers slightly more, I had decided to place in front of each of them a critic who expounded his own point of view on the same phenomenon. These inner and outer perspectives generally converged and their complementarity threw a vivid light on the mystery of artistic creation. That was the purpose of this meeting. It is also the aim of this book.

I.

IRISH POETS
AND
THE CREATIVE PROCESS

THE FRONTIER OF WRITING

Seamus Heaney

Everything that can be usefully said about poetic composition
has been said already, so my remarks on the subject make no
claim to originality. And since I believe that there is a better
chance of establishing credible first principles in this area by
dealing with writings and writers from the traditional canon, I
want to begin with a poem by Thomas Hardy: 'Afterwards'.

> When the Present has latched its postern behind my
>   tremulous stay,
> And the May month flaps its glad green leaves like wings,
> Delicate-filmed as new-spun silk, will the neighbours say,
> 'He was a man who used to notice such things?'
>
> If it be in the dusk when, like an eyelid's soundless blink,
> The dewfall-hawk comes crossing the shades to alight
> Upon the wind-warped upland thorn, a gazer may think,
> 'To him this must have been a familiar sight.'
>
> If I pass during some nocturnal blackness, mothy and warm,
> When the hedgehog travels furtively over the lawn,
> One may say, 'He strove that such innocent creatures should
>   come to no harm,
> But he could do little for them; and now he is gone.'
>
> If, when hearing that I have been stilled at last, they stand
>   at the door,
> Watching the full-starred heavens that winter sees,
> Will this thought rise on those who will meet my face no more,
> 'He was one who had an eye for such mysteries.'

And will any say when my bell of quittance is heard
   in the gloom
And a crossing breeze cuts a pause in its outrollings,
Till they rise again, as they were a new bell's boom,
'He hears it not now, but used to notice such things?'

To state the obvious: this is a poem in which the poet contemplates the prospect of his death, and manages to view that prospect with a certain equanimity. He comes across as somebody who knows that he will end up as a piece of conversational flotsam, a desultory if warmly regarded item in the community's store of recollections. So, from one point of view, Hardy's 'Afterwards' is an embrace of the untransfigured ordinary, an act of solidarity with the usual world where people stand in their doorways, wistful rather than desolate at the news of a death, and repeat the conventional decencies. 'He was a man who used to notice such things. To him this must have been a familiar sight. Now he is gone.'

This acknowledgement of the untransfigured, repetitive and typical nature of human lives and deaths is one of the real strengths of the poem, but it is by no means the only one. For 'Afterwards' is not just another poignant treatment of the theme of human mortality; it is also a dramatic revelation of the way human language can amplify and outlive that mortality – which is to say that in the end the poem is more given over to the extraordinary than to the ordinary, more devoted to the superabundance of the imagined response than to the adequacy of the actual social one. It is a poem which does indeed contemplate the prospect of its writer's death, but more importantly, it manifests the world-renewing potential of his writing. In each of its stanzas, reader and writer cross a line which divides the country of conventional utterance from the country of total expressiveness, a frontier between the transports of fluency and the limitations of social speech. And this initiation into copiousness and superabundant rightness constitutes an initiation into poetry itself, which is always over and above, always (as Keats declared) surprising by a fine excess.

'He was a man who used to notice such things,' say the neighbours on one side of the frontier. 'Which things?' asks the reader. 'That the May-month flaps its glad green leaves like wings, / Delicate filmed as new-spun silk,' says the poem from the other side of the frontier. 'To him this must have been a familiar sight,' say the neighbours. 'Which sight?' says the reader. 'The dusk, when like an eyelid's soundless blink, / The dewfall hawk comes crossing the shades to alight / Upon the wind-warped upland thorn,' says the poem. 'Anything else?' says the reader. 'Blackness, mothy and warm,' says the poem, 'the hedgehog travelling furtively over the lawn, the full-starred heavens that winter sees, and so on,' says the poem. 'My God,' says the reader.

The poem is a showing forth of the way that poetry brings human existence into a fuller life. If it is less extravagant in its gestures than Rilke's 'Sonnets to Orpheus', it is no less fully alive to the excitements and transformations which poetic activity promotes. In fact, we could bend to our purpose here the words which conclude Rilke's first sonnet in the Orpheus sequence; we could say that the opening lines of each of the five stanzas of 'Afterwards' 'make a temple deep inside our hearing,' a temple which stands on the other side of the divide created by the passage of the god of poetry himself.

The best moments in a writer's life are when this kind of thing happens, during those bouts of composition when he or she or the poem itself seems to be walking on air; those moments when the poem has a wildness and yet a subject is also being fulfilled. These are terms used by Robert Frost in his essay 'The Figure a Poem Makes', where he also speaks about 'unexpected supply' and 'remembering something I didn't know I knew'.

My own image for this entry into writerly bliss is symptomatic of a Northern Irish Catholic background, but no less interesting for that, I hope. A poet, after all, is born out of the social as well as the psychic conditions. At any rate, it often seems to me that the crossing of the lyric barrier bears a certain resemblance to the experience (common in Ulster) of getting through a road-block or a border checkpoint manned by the British army. These are thresholds that you approach with a slight mounting of anxiety and that you get through with a primitive delight in being set free. Perhaps the neurosis is peculiar to the minority in Northern Ireland, but in those casually military conditions, one's freedom and self-confidence are under threat and the inclination to confine oneself to a minimal, conventional speech is instinctive. The formal interrogation and presentation of driver's license, the wait and inspection of the car, the consultation at the roadside by the attendant police or soldiers – it all combines to remind you of the vulnerability of your situation. If your name is Seamus, you have known from childhood that you are marked by that name as one of the suspected and that feeling of having something to answer for is reinforced by the fact you are now being investigated anyhow. So these constricting forces – which in life are the results of various political and social impositions, internalized and accommodated – these constrictions can represent the repressions and self-censorings which hamper a writer and keep him or her stalled at the barrier of composition.

But there is another moment, a moment of gratifying permission when the license is handed back, you are waved on, the brake and clutch release, the gears get purchase, and everything is on the move again – and in my allegory that moment represents the beginning of the slide into fluency which initiates poetic composition. So, in the poem that I wrote about all of this, the roadblock is described twice, first as an incident on a journey and then as an occasion recollected and transformed by the writing. The poem is called 'From the Frontier of Writing':

> The tightness and the nilness round that space
> when the car stops in the road, the troops inspect
> its make and number and, as one bends his face
>
> towards the window, you catch sight of more
> on a hill beyond, eyeing with intent
> down cradled guns that hold you under cover
>
> and everything is pure interrogation
> until a rifle motions and you move
> with guarded unconcerned acceleration –
>
> a little emptier, a little spent
> as always by that quiver in the self,
> subjugated, yes, and obedient . . .
>
> So you drive on to the frontier of writing
> where it happens again. The guns on tripods;
> the sergeant with his on-off mike repeating
>
> data about you, waiting for the squawk
> of clearance; the marksman training down
> out of the sun upon you like a hawk.

And suddenly you're through, arraigned yet freed,
as if you'd passed from behind a waterfall
on the black current of a tarmac road

past armour-plated vehicles, out between
the posted soldiers flowing and receding
like tree shadows into the polished windscreen.

In recent years, when I have been asked to talk about the activity of lyric poetry, this image, or something like it, has kept recurring. What I am seeking is a way to illustrate the fact that lyric writing always involves the shifting of a weight of personal experience through a certain distance. I am attracted to this notion for several reasons, not least because it brings the work of art within the scope of a definition of work which applies to work of every other sort. What was taught in school as a formula – the old equation which said that work equalled the product of the mass moved multiplied by the distance it travelled – that now seems to me to be a perfectly apt description of what happens when a poem *works*. In a poem, the load of the world is not abandoned or absconded from; it is more that by application of imaginative force it is set in motion, and once it is in motion, it feels lighter and more manageable; it is still recognizably *a weight* but the weight is no longer a dead weight. A poem shifts the constituent parts of a world into a new co-ordination. For all the lines of force which pull it down and back, there are equal and opposite lines which boost it up and away, and the special gift of poetry is precisely that salubrious feeling of having the best of both worlds.

These ideas gained new validity for me when I wrote some poems that were a very definite reaction against the kind of deliberately unlyrical work I did in the title poem of *Station Island* (1984). When I completed *Station Island*, a natural lightening and release seemed to occur, and the first result of it was a group of poems published as a sequence under the title 'Sweeney Redivivus'. These were written quickly and confidently, each one a kind of swoop upon some occasion or predicament of my own life, but conducted from the perspective of a liberated, exorcised consciousness, a consciousness that I identified with that of Mad Sweeney. During the 1970s I had translated and dwelt upon Sweeney's story until he had become a kind of subjective correlative, so once I surrendered my lumpy, earthbound autobiographical self to his giddier, more extravagant and more pre-emptive voice, I felt the old pleasurable drag and lift of crossing the frontier by the airbridge of awakened language.

In these poems, I was not assuming Sweeney's identity. I was not attempting to write dramatic monologues for him, or placing him realistically in an early medieval setting. But neither was the 'I' of the writing just my own first-person-singular identity, co-terminous with my social and historical experience. Even if I had not disappeared *into* Sweeney, I had still got beyond myself: a shift had happened and that which I had previously known as a matter of my own experience had been moved to a point where it felt like a recognition by another consciousness. Each poem came into being as a thrown shape. The actual writing involved a quick jump into the current of possibility, as if the Sweeney figure were a kind of imaginary surfboard upon which you took your chances to ride the current of association as far as it would go. I couldn't say, for example, whether the voice that speaks in the following poem is more energized by the fiction of Sweeney, the volatile, exiled king, half-glad to be shot of the world he once belonged to and half-dependent upon it for his meaning in the world he was banished to – I couldn't say whether there's more of that fictitious Sweeney in the voice, or more of my own memory of being in Wicklow in the mid-seventies, having split from Belfast a few years earlier and ended up in what another Sweeney-crossed poem called 'a migrant solitude'. Here, at any rate, from 'Sweeney Redivivus' is the poem 'The First Flight':

> It was more sleepwalk than spasm
> yet that was a time when the times
> were also in spasm –
>
> the ties and the knots running through us
> split open
> down the lines of the grain.
>
> As I drew close to pebbles and berries,
> the smell of wild garlic, relearning
> the acoustic of frost
>
> and the meaning of woodnote,
> my shadow over the field
> was only a spin-off,

my empty place an excuse
for shifts in the camps, old rehearsals
of debts and betrayal.

Singly they came to the tree
with a stone in each pocket
to whistle and bill me back in

and I would collide and cascade
through leaves when they left,
my point of repose knocked askew.

I was mired in attachment
until they began to pronounce me
a feeder of battlefields

so I mastered new rungs of the air
to survey out of reach
their bonfires on hills, their hosting

and fasting, the levies from Scotland
as always, and the people of art
diverting their rhythmical chants

to fend off the onslaught of winds
I would welcome and climb
at the top of my bent.

As I say, this was neither straight autobiography nor sheer fiction. It swam into my ken, like Sweeney, between the headiness of the air and the bother on the ground; but what made the writing of it so liberating was the very fact that the writing did move, that it shifted the 1970s situation into the early mediaeval phantasmagoria, that the lines were more alive to their possibility as language play than to their responsibilities as documentary of any sort.

The constant problem for every poet is to find a way to initiate this process of transition from the world of data to the words of invention. How is the conventional understanding of things to be resolved into something new and vividly rendered? How to get from the usual tongue-tied apprehension of ordinary things in terms such as the neighbours of 'Afterwards' would employ – how to get from that to the untrammelled and effortlessly resourceful speech available in the poem itself? The American poet-critic, Robert Pinsky, answers these questions succinctly and decisively in an essay in his recent book, *Poetry and the World*. 'In some ways,' Pinsky writes,

before the artist can see a subject – foreign policy or any other subject – the artist must transform it: answer the received cultural imagination of the subject with something utterly different. This need to answer by transforming is primary. . . . The poet needs to feel utterly free, yet answerable.

'Answer the received cultural imagination of the subject with something completely different.' That is a wonderfully simple statement of a complex and unforceable process, the kind of thing that happens in John Montague's poem 'The Grafted Tongue', when he answers the nineteenth century language shift in Ireland with the fact of his stammer; and it also applies to the story of a significant writing experience that I want to tell before drawing these remarks to a close. I want to spend the rest of the time talking about the way a piece of artwork on the gable of the Guinness Hop Store in Dublin started off a process of composition which did, I think, answer the received cultural imagination of a subject with something completely different. A conventional account of this subject would call it 'the new Ireland,' the Euro-Ireland of high-rise offices and expense account lunches, press conferences and image-making, an Ireland still caught between the lure of an old religious sense of reality and the promptings of a new self-interested opportunistic way of life. An Ireland with an archaic unconscious and a gift for chic adaptation. An Ireland half-proud that it has shed old taboos and superstitions, yet half-afraid that it has thereby cast itself adrift from an essential moral and spiritual anchorage.

All of these ways of speaking do indeed represent what Pinsky calls 'the received cultural imagination of the subject', but they have little in common with a mandala of muddy hand prints on a high wall in Dublin at a Rosc exhibition in the summer of 1986. This was an artwork carried out by the English artist Richard Long, and it consisted of a huge display of concentric circles high on a whitewashed wall, each circle made up of hand prints and each hand print made with mud. The whole image was simultaneously buoyant and sluggish, the circular elevation of it somehow suggestive of heavenly visitation, while the muddy textures of it represented forces that were earthbound and creaturely. It was like a cathedral window celebrating earthiness rather than airiness, an apparition out of the immanent rather than transcendent. At any rate, it moved and answered all at once; it presented itself dreamily to my mind as a kind of counter-apparition, to apparitions of the sort that still happen every now and again in Ireland – when the Virgin Mary turns up unexpectedly on the gable of a local church or in the branches of a hawthorn bush at the foot of somebody's garden.

I had lived through such an event myself during the late 1950s, when the Mother of God was supposed to have appeared to a woman in Ardboe, in Co. Tyrone. I was then in my late teens and was both susceptible to the mood of excitement which was running through the whole district, if also a bit sceptical about it. My susceptibility, moreover, derived from a sense of miracle and a sensation of fear that I had experienced years before the Ardboe event, when I had attended a play done by schoolchildren in our local hall. This had been a sort of pageant about the apparitions of the Virgin Mary at Fatima in Portugal, and I can still recollect the frisson I experienced night after night when a rickety lighting device blazed into action, and green and crimson filters made lurid swirls all over the stage – all meant to represent the reported miracle when the sun was said to have changed colour so that an atheistical journalist had there and then fallen on his knees and been converted. None of this, of course, was in my mind when I drove with my parents to the site of the action in Ardboe, yet there was an equivalent sense of occasion, a real mounting of expectation as we approached the place and people began to appear like pilgrims on the road, walking in ones and twos. Fields and lanes were full of parked cars and buses, so that it was like approaching a football field in the country when a game was in progress; except that here, instead of spectator shouts, there was an eerie hush. Then, as you pushed in closer to the locus of expectation, the hush became a murmur of prayers, and the prayers and litanies became a mantra invoking Mary to pray for us, pray for us, pray for us, now and at the hour of our death.

As I looked up at the mudprints Richard Long had put on the wall of the Hop Store, I began to imagine them standing on their own against the sky, an apparition every bit as numinous as those I've just been describing, but one whose significance would have to be invented by me – so already I was on the move towards the frontier of writing. I began to connect this earthy sign which I'd imagined in the Irish air with de Valera's dream of transforming the local customs and folk Catholicism of rural Ireland in the middle of the twentieth century into something more self-conscious and purposeful, his dream of founding a culturally distinct and spiritually resistant Irish republic, a dream which has been gradually abandoned without ever being replaced by any alternative vision of the future, certainly not by anything as ardent or self-born. Not that I was very clear about how the parallels were going to be drawn between the image and the historical conditions: it all just hung there in the misty element of the preconscious mind like something in a murky solution about to crystallize, and it was only when I surrendered to the slightly loony logic of the fiction that the possibilities began to unfold. And, as in the case of the Sweeney poem I read earlier, when the writing did start to flow it was impossible to say whether the historical background or the imagined story had a more determining effect upon the progress and outcome of the poem itself. Here, at any rate, is what I eventually wrote:

THE MUD VISION

Statues with exposed hearts and barbed-wire crowns
Still stood in alcoves, hares flitted beneath
The dozing bellies of jets, our menu-writers
And punks with aerosol sprays held their own
With the best of them. Satellite link-ups
Wafted over us the blessings of popes, heliports
Maintained a charmed circle for idols on tour
And casualties on their stretchers. We sleepwalked
The line between panic and formulae, screen-tested
Our first native models and the last of the mummers,
Watching ourselves at a distance, advantaged
And airy as a man on a springboard
Who keeps limbering up because the man cannot dive.

And then in the foggy midlands it appeared,
Our mud vision, as if a rose window of mud
Had invented itself out of the glittery damp,
A gossamer wheel, concentric with its own hub
Of nebulous dirt, sullied yet lucent.
We had heard of the sun standing still and the sun
That changed colour, but we were vouchsafed
Original clay, transfigured and spinning.

And then the sunsets ran murky, the wiper
Could never entirely clean off the windscreen,
Reservoirs tasted of silt, a light fuzz
Accrued in the hair and the eyebrows, and some
Took to wearing a smudge on their forehead
To be prepared for whatever, Vigils
Began to be kept around puddled gaps,
On altars bulrushes ousted the lilies
And a rota of invalids came and went
On beds they could lease placed in range of the shower.

A generation who had seen a sign!
Those nights when we stood in an umber dew and smelled
Mould in the verbena, or woke to a light
Furrow-breath on the pillow, when the talk
Was all about who had seen it and our fear
Was touched with a secret pride, only ourselves
Could be adequate then to our lives. When the rainbow
Curved flood-brown and ran like a water-rat's back
So that drivers on the hard-shoulder switched off to watch,
We wished it away, and yet we presumed it a test
That would prove us beyond expectation.

We lived, of course, to learn the folly of that.
One day it was gone and the east gable
Where its trembling corolla had balanced
Was starkly a ruin again, with dandelions
Blowing high up on the ledges, and moss
That slumbered on through its increase. As cameras raked
The site from every angle, experts
Began their post factum jabber and all of us
Crowded in tight for the big explanations.
Just like that, we forgot that the vision was ours,
Our one chance to know the incomparable
And dive to a future. What might have been origin
We dissipated in news. The clarified place
Had retrieved neither us nor itself – except
You could say we survived. So say that, and watch us
Who had our chance to be mud-men, convinced and estranged,
Figure in our own eyes for the eyes of the world.

* * *

In the end, of course, what is sweetest and strangest about lyric writing is the pre-verbal operation of the psyche – what has been called the dream-work. This rich and remotely controlling prehistory of the poem is something that can neither be consciously prepared nor entirely accounted for, yet it is the essential power source upon which the poem depends. When a poem begins to move with an energy of its own, when the writer begins to feel that which Frost calls 'the wonder of unexpected supply', when the sensation of being on a moving stair or a bridge of air or a surfboard begins to take over, then we can be fairly sure that a preconscious source is giving power from below. And so it turned out to be in the case of that catherine wheel of mud prints. Months afterwards, I realised that Richard Long's image corresponded deeply to one of my own very first experiences of sheer delight, an experience of complete agogness and rapture which I had consciously sought and deliberately created and recreated when I was a child. Within the wheels of the concentric circles of Long's painting and within the wheels of my imagined rose window of mud, there was another wheel, the actual, spinning back wheel of a bicycle; and this actual wheel had then gradually turned itself into one of those flywheels at the very hub of memory itself. Here, therefore, are the first two sections of a poem I wrote later and published in *Seeing Things* (1987) called 'Wheels within Wheels':

> The first real grip I ever got on things
> Was when I learned the art of pedalling
> (By hand) a bike turned upside down, and drove
> Its back wheel preternaturally fast.
> I loved the disappearance of the spokes,
> The way the space between the hub and rim
> Hummed with transparency. If you threw
> A potato into it, the hooped air
> Spun mush and drizzle back into your face;
> If you touched it with a straw, the straw frittered.
> Something about the way those pedal treads
> Worked very palpably at first against you
> And then began to sweep your hand ahead
> Into a new momentum – that all entered me
> Like an access of free power, as if belief
> Caught up and spun the objects of belief
> In an orbit coterminous with longing.

But enough was not enough. Who ever saw
The limit in the given anyhow?
In fields beyond our house there was a well
('The well' we called it. It was more a hole
With water in it, with small hawthorn trees
On one side, and a muddy, dungy ooze
On the other, all tramped through by cattle).
I loved that too. I loved the turbid smell,
The sump-life of the place like old chain oil.
And there, next thing, I brought my bicycle.
I stood its saddle and its handlebars
Into the soft bottom, I touched the tyres
To the water's surface, then turned the pedals
Until like a mill-wheel pouring at the treadles
(But here reversed and lashing a mare's tail)
The world-refreshing and immersed back wheel
Spun lace and dirt-suds there before my eyes
And showered me in my own regenerate clays.
For weeks I made a nimbus of old glit.
Then the hub jammed, rims rusted, the chain snapped.

This is a direct account of the experience which worked itself indirectly into 'The Mud Vision'. The world-refreshing lens of the back wheel of that bicycle had sailed like a dream frisbee across the frontier of writing and dawned on the adult consciousness as a kind of solar summons to the imagination.

In a poem, in other words, we move ahead of ourselves in order to arrive at that which was inside us all the time. So I will conclude with a very brief piece which moves from one side of the frontier to the other inside two lines. This couplet is a mini-parable about the necessity of bringing the world across the divide which Hardy's 'Afterwards' acknowledges, the divide separating the neighbours' outwardness from the poet's inwardness; in other words, this poem is also a celebration of the totally satisfactory nature of the totally imagined experience. It is based on a memory of a quiet afternoon in a graveyard in Yorkshire, during which we went to stand beneath trees at the edge of the church grounds. We had gone across to listen to a river which we could hear flowing there, but gradually realized that the river was dry at that time of the summer and what we were attending to – with the kind of complete attention that the creatures gave to the song of Orpheus – was the sound of wind in the branches. The poem says in seconds what I have been striving to say in perhaps too many different ways throughout this paper:

> The riverbed, dried up, half-full of leaves.

> Us, listening to a river in the trees.

SEAMUS HEANEY AND THE GENTLE FLAME

Maurice Harmon

The poetry in Seamus Heaney's first three collections – *Death of a Naturalist* (1966), *Door into the Dark* (1969), *Wintering Out* 1972 – seems to be a poetry of happy recovery in which the imagination repossesses a secure, familiar background. Deceptively, it transcends the divide that education and departure have made between the self that writes and the self that is written about. That need to create an imaginative world in between what was and what is, or between what is and what the imagination prefers, runs throughout Heaney's career. In these early books he creates an attractive place with the materials of an actual place.

To speak of the early poetry only in terms of happy relationship is to miss the tensions out of which it grows. The creative consciousness works across a division between understanding and experience. The poet has been distanced from the things which were a natural part of his formative years. To miss the disruption and uncertainty caused by that loss, and the resulting need to discover and fashion an individual identity, is to undervalue the struggle from which the poetry comes. The poetry makes up for loss, refuses to be defeated, works out an attractive interpretation of the past and in the process commemorates a way of life and a Wordsworthian fostering by beauty and fear. It strengthens the connection, is self-strengthening and self-creating, a forging of values through a process of sympathetic reckoning. The poetry defines what he values in his former community and in that definition defines and demonstrates its own values – those of craft and of belonging, of being in touch with and true to a place, what it has produced and what it has gone through.

17

If we take 'Digging' as the moment in which the poet first feels what he may do, we can take 'Bogland' as the first direction-finder out of the familiar. 'Bogland's' idealised landscape ratifies what the imagination holds dear. The choice taken seems to exclude the road not taken, the one, in effect, Heaney actually took. The more successful he was in creating a viable past the more conscious he became of all that separated him from it. At the same time, the world that he took as his imagination's domain in the mid-Sixties was, within two or three years, afflicted by the recurrence of Northern Troubles. These, too, had to be faced; the signs of that coming storm could be read in the landscape.

Poems that take linguistic soundings read the landscape but also define its divisions between Planter and Gael, Protestant and Catholic, Unionist and Nationalist. There is a legacy of injustice and fear. The poetry's beauty of sound and shape substitutes but does not deny the dissonance of political division, dispossession, colonisation and loss. At the deepest level the poems fight back, saying that deprivation cannot, will not, deny the poet the fullest possible imaginative achievement. That claim is subtly presented, the more tellingly present for being conveyed within image, metaphor and sound. Resentment, nationalist hurt, and racial wrong are driving forces. Some poems evoke an ancestry beyond Tudor invasion and plantation. Some fire warning shots across the gates of the demesne. The Moyola poems are detonations underground, where rivers run deep. Their explosive power is all the greater for being so melodious. In these ways Heaney finds a resolution to the challenges of his background and culture, to the heritage of dispossession, to personal memories of injustice, and of being made feel inferior, in a culture where one's very name evokes a political-religious coloration. He also takes a political stand without being drawn into the rhetoric of politics. The poetry grows from his struggle with himself, from his discovery, acceptance and creation of his fated field.

If he was to accept his responsibility as a poet who was drawn, as 'Bogland' makes clear, towards a full investigation of its layered, complex, divided nature, he would find a means by which to investigate it. *Wintering Out* (1972) as well as taking soundings, took stock. In its examination of heritage, he sides with the mound-dwellers, the last mummer, the servant boy who draws him into his trail. The servant boy knows the back doors of the little barons; he has developed a way of dealing with historical injustice; he keeps his patience and his counsel, is 'resentful and impenitent'. Behind him lie the causes of his condition: plantations, poverty, starvation, the 'geniuses who creep' in Spenser's terrible account. Like the last mummer, Heaney is 'trammelled / in the taboos of the country', picks his way through 'the long toils of blood / and feuding', is adaptable and self-protective. The language anticipates the verbal landscape of *North*.

In the extensive investigation of how the self feels, and how the self responds to a situation that is in itself not simple, the poetry creates a variety of mirroring presences; not just the man hooped to his fields, not just the music-makers with their ears to the ground, but the servant boy, the mummer, the dispossessed. He is 'snared' to the land he has composed habits for. He is 'hooped', 'sleeved', hides in the hollow trunk, Ireland is his nation, he speaks in a self-identifying way in a place where speech reveals who you are. He registers all of this, claims it all, acknowledges it all. He will not shirk or disguise both what attracts and what seems alien. The poems respond to the tug and pull of a divided heritage which he does not simplify; the more he explores it, the more richly and variously can it be realised. He can opt for an attractive reading of place names, since these verify what he is. He yields to a self-defining impulse. 'I opened my right-of-way', 'I composed habits', 'I was ready to go anywhere', 'I might turn', 'I just make out', 'I cock an ear', 'I would question', 'I push in', 'I am sleeved'. In these projections of an investigative, identifying pioneer, he negotiates his way in the layered landscape. The servant boy is also the watching poet in 'A New Song'. In 'The Other Side', the dispossessed speak and observe: language both identifies and divides. On the other side the chosen people, the promised land, the bible; on his side the poor land, the scraggy acres, the mournful rosary. There is, to be sure, a kind of farming community that can overlook these divisions, but what happens when that neighbour puts on the uniform of an armed B-Special, mans checks points on the roads, interrogates, and asserts control? How does that experience affect the servant boy, the last mummer, the men with the memories of ancient wrongs of which this is just the immediate sign? In 'The Constable Calls' the law is male, dominating, and frightening. The 'Docker's' fist would drop a hammer on a Catholic. There are more ways than one of keeping your independence. The navvy has not relented, he is plugged to the hard core. Heaney's road has more twists and dips to it, it accommodates a freer way of going. In the late Sixties the hammer began to fall and has been falling ever since.

Poetry occurs somewhere between dreaming and thinking. Much that goes on is instinctive and unpremeditated. Poets trust secret tributaries that, at times, flow together, meeting and consorting agreeably. Much of Heaney's water music is a tribute to the process. So are several poems in *North* (1975) which repeat the emphatic self-defining drive. What he needed and what he found was a metaphor to illuminate his accumulated awareness of the North's politics. Reading Glob's *Bog People* engendered an intellectual and imaginative scheme: a pagan religion comparable to Christianity, a myth of killing and resurrection, the images of Tollund Man, Grauballe Man, and others, more vivid than the images of Christ or the saints in the familiar texts; parallels between early Iron Age atrocities, and similar deeds carried out in Northern Ireland. The manner of writing poems which echoed with cultural, racial, and historical definition is replaced with a more explicit moral definition. The 'we' and the 'our' of poems that were admissions of happy belonging, give way to a more troubled reflection on complicity as well as belonging. When the violence affects and involves your kith and kin, you are also involved, even though you never fire a shot. When your poetry responds to historical wrong you are involved. Ironically, because the poetic evidence of your sympathy is embodied in image and metaphor, those who would claim you as theirs and with whom you feel closely bound may be dissatisfied with what you write. 'Now they will say I bite the hand that fed me'. You also question yourself. To what degree and in what ways may you comment directly on political violence? Where does your responsibility to life end and your responsibility to art begin? What separates the two? You experience and suffer a dual loyalty. You may seek a solution to that division, but the solution is never clear-cut.

The poems in *North* look into the self not out from the self. They are self-examining pilgrimages into the conscience. In rough outline they may be seen to animate a shifting drama of response, with different personae, different scenes. They animate his involvement. 'I touch it again', 'I wind it in', 'I push back through dictions' . . . 're-enter memory', 'I hold my lady's head / like a crystal'. 'I unpin', 'I unwrap' . . . 'and see'. 'I reach past'. Within the portrait of two cultures they enact a variety of ways in which to reflect both worlds, and to use the two in mutually revealing exposure. They test the appropriateness of his reaction, release his delight in what works, remind him of the dangers in the comparison, recognise its evasive, voyeuristic aspects, and condemn what he does. 'Funeral Rites' wills itself towards the slow triumph of the bonding, comforting funeral. It leads to the image of Gunnar in a state of blessedness beyond revenge, where the cycle of violence has ended. 'North's' epiphany is the savagery he has transcended. In a self-dramatising mime, 'Viking Dublin: Trial Pieces' identifies the poet as a moralist sniffing out corruption. He shows us the Vikings for what they are: hoarders of grudges, killers, gombeenmen. In 'The Bog Queen', the victim rises from the dark and speaks directly. 'The Grauballe Man' inspects a victim so perfected that he does not seem to be a corpse. In 'Punishment', the most self-accusing of the poems, the empathetic imagination is even more intimate. 'I would have cast, . . . / the stones of silence'. 'I would have stood dumb'

> connive
> in civilized outrage
> yet understand the exact
> and tribal, intimate revenge.

In 'Strange Fruit' the beheaded girl outstares atrocity and the poet's stylised transmutation. 'Kinship' celebrates the bog under its various aspects. 'This centre holds'. 'I grew out of all this'. He was also Hamlet the Dane, parablist, and so on. 'Ocean's Love to Ireland', and related poems, give the historical background of possession and dispossession. He 'defied' memories of his own life, but this is our land; we have savage ways, too. Evenhandedly, scapegoat, victim, divided witness, the poet suffers, digests, and creates love and horror.

Heaney's work, the poetry, the articles, interviews, reviews, essays, and uncollected poems, reveal conflict and uncertainty. There are inconsistencies and contradictions, what he says on one occasion qualified by what he says on another, the choices made in one book of poems qualified by options taken in another, perceptions in one section of a book qualified by perceptions in another. The poems enact and share a drama of decision and indecision. The poet writes to see himself, his situation and its possibilities, to open doors into the light of the rational imagination, as well as into the dark interior of the self. He reaches out in discovery and intuition, returns to what was already perceived and recovered, enters into it in a deeper exploration to feel renewed and newly validated. He is always a pilgrim back into the land of the self and its contexts, always a searcher after secret word-hoards who expands the sense of conflict and pain in the hinterland and in himself. He re-enacts what has made him and in that re-enactment finds himself. But it is not an uninterrupted, error-free line of development. It is unfair to draw over him, in misguided admiration, a chart of constant growth and development. Such praise leaves out the struggle through which and by which the poetry and growth take place.

In *North* by adopting the voice of the victim or by celebrating the redeeming processes of the bog, Heaney avoids stating directly and simplistically how he feels. He also releases language from the kind of inertness that a response to immediate horror may induce. It is the bog queen who narrates her story; it is the Viking dead who become things of beauty. By analogy present horror is subsumed. The method sweetens savagery. Playful submission to the forces of the bog distances atrocity and produces the risen beauty. But the tone changes: the mother ground is sour with the blood of her faithful; we slaughter for the common good, shave the heads of the notorious, 'the goddess swallows / our love and terror'. The imagination digests whatever comes.

Whereas Part 1 of *North* creates a world beside the real world, mirroring it but apart, Part 11 marks the presence of policemen, politicians, journalists, orange drums, sectarianism, and cute evasion. Its dates mark a personal sequence of confusion, uncertainty, fear, inferiorities induced by church and state, and the stirrings of individuality. There is the characteristic note of unease: 'for all this art and sedentary trade / I am incapable'. The voice, too, wavers: it expresses communal irritation.

The poems lead on to 'Exposure' where in wintry weather, the poet questions his responsibility. This is self-definition of a kind not attempted before in all the placings of the mimetic self, the histrionic imagination cauled in history, or geography, or language. Instead of certainties it poses questions. How and why did he end up like this, both victim and witness, sharing Mandlestam's *tristia*? Now the Viking dead speak with forked tongues. The scales are balanced. The imagined hero stands for a simplicity that will not work in a complex situation. There is no place for the once in a lifetime deed. But there are other virtues such as endurance, patience, precision, and wisdom in the face of sadness. And there is, as the poem itself demonstrates, as do *North*, *Field Work* and *Station Island*, the virtue of honest, balanced reckoning. This quietness is a strength, because it says what all good poems say, that poetry has force by virtue of its own truth.

In 1974 Heaney said that the poet's function was not to help people to adapt to the Northern crisis or to overcome it. His role was to give a true picture of man's inhumanity to man, and for that he found the Icelandic sagas a good parallel, 'dealing as they did with a tightly knit community, reciprocal feuding and murders which did not shock anyone too badly'.[1] The shock is absorbed through poetry, filtered in the imaginative treatment. Gunnar is a beautiful image, but the vengeance in fact continued. Art can create images of beauty to transcend and transmute blood and death. But that achievement is not a form of callous indifference. Just because the poems in *North* become objects of beauty, absorbing suffering and death, and just because he places one world beside another, does not mean that the poet does not suffer with the people. He is both Antaeus and Hercules. The experiences that punish them, the atrocities, deaths, imprisonments, violence, fear, frustration, also enter him. What he does is to digest and reuse this savage food, refusing to meet savagery with a brutal response. That would demean poetry and the poet. Instead, he creates things of beauty in the belief that beautiful objects satisfy and soothe.

Field Work (1979) has a cutting edge. The poems outline a world that has its enduring simplicities and pieties, its solid beauty of object and task. But violence intrudes: soldiers patrolling where they do not belong, young men with guns on the hillsides, intimations of violence, questions of survival, the need for forgiveness and understanding; 'the island is full of comfortless voices'. 'Who's sorry for our trouble?' 'What will become of us?' Was the fisherman in 'Casualty' culpable? 'How perilous is it to choose / Not to love the things we're shown?' 'What is my apology for poetry?' Questioning is now a mode as well as a mood. The voice is close to the poet's actual voice. The drama of self-perception is more intense. The artist-fisherman is true to impulses and allegiances that must not be overruled. In poem after poem the artist goes about his business. That justification has to be made in the face of conflicting pressures between art and life. For example, how should the poet have reacted when his cousin was shot?

Heaney was deeply troubled by the suffering and self-sacri-
fice of the hunger-strikers. They were victims as much as those
in the early Iron Age. If he could react sympathetically to them,
could he not react with equal sympathy to these nearer home?
Might he be too scrupulous in refusing to get involved? He felt
the urge to respond, but to do so, he argued, is to lose one's
mystery by being too openly part of a political situation. He was
caught 'between the urge to write lyric poetry, to make beautiful
things that are comforting' and the parallel desire to 'wreck that
comfort' with the poet's truth.[2] But the truth of art is a different
truth. Nevertheless, the demands on him cannot easily be pushed
aside. Is he too self-conscious in his unease about the poet's role
in the circumstances? To shut out politics would in itself be a
political statement. To write lyrics at a time of deep suffering
may give the impression that it is not all that important. He
looked at other poets.

Yeats took a stand. In 'Easter 1916' he declared himself in
relation to an event and a period. Dante placed himself within
history, and addressed public events in a forceful way. The evidence showed that a poet could speak confidently out of a
particular history and a particular set of circumstances. His personal dilemmas may be focused where history and the individual
life intersect. *Field Work* brings the autobiographical self into immediate contact with particular individuals, whose lives have
been brutally and wastefully ended in a situation with which
Heaney has always identified. The contact is on the level of
kinship, shared experience and an intimate relationship with the
common landscape. Tenderness and immediacy, plainness of language and feeling characterise these portraits of individuals
fatally caught in the realities of history, in Heaney's time and
place.

Literature itself is a form of betrayal. At a remove from experience it substitutes fictions for experience, and exposes what
might prefer to be hidden. It can comment on politics without
becoming directly involved. Again Yeats is an example. Being so
aware of the causes and consequences of violence in the North,
Heaney could easily feel guilty of evasion. In *Station Island* (1984)
we hear the doubting self. The dead accuse: 'You confused evasion with artistic tact'. Heaney pleads: 'forgive my timid
circumstantial involvement' and judges 'I hate everything / That
made me biddable and unforthcoming'. At the same time he
must be free, must have his own imaginative space, to fill as he

will with the 'trial pieces' of his art. That is the absolution he seeks.

Station Island re-examines forces, people, incidents, memories. In one frame after another it delineates moments of significant experience. Its series of encounters create a complex, changing and developing drama of identification, involvement and assessment. 'You have to try to make sense of what comes'. You have to 'remember everything and keep your head'. Some are tender revisitings, some evoke known places, or remembered objects; these are 'refreshing'. Feeling and love are essential to the poet-pilgrim's examination of things past and present: not flinty purpose, but compassion, sympathy and understanding, virtues appropriate to a pilgrimage, and to a poem. No longer assertive the I figure reviews, acknowledges, confesses. Confession is not just about guilt, or the burdens of poetic responsibility.

The accusing voices are deeply challenging. The murdered cousin, for example, subject of the Lough Beg elegy, brings forward the conflict between suffering and lyric poetry. The elegy concludes with a soothing ceremony: 'I dab you clean', 'I lift you under the arms and lay you flat', 'I plait / Green scapulars to wear over your shroud' – The tone is direct and intimate. When Heaney wrote in pity, he did not express anger at the murder, nor did he voice the rage of a people suffering such outrage. Carleton could wield the knife of sectarian hatred, but Heaney will not wield the 'unforgiving iron'. The agitated voice of the next victim relives love and terror, the horror of sectarian violence, his doomed walk to face his bare-faced killers. This death is not veiled in lyric song. The voice is ferocious. It confronts the poet's 'circumspect involvement'. The victim simply does not understand the poet's choice and that makes the choice harder to justify.

Heaney responds: 'Forgive the way I have lived indifferent'. Faced with the death of the archaeologist he admits another failure – the failure to comfort. Ironically, the poet who can provide solace in poetry, cannot bring comfort to his dying friend: he felt 'guilty and empty'; he had 'failed an obligation'; is struck dumb. He was struck dumb also at the news of his cousin's death; his feelings dried up. But the cousin dismisses such explanation, accuses him of confusing evasion with artistic tact, of whitewashing ugliness, of making death sweet with the saccharine of his poetry, and this also hurts. Faced with the figure of a

Maze hunger-striker, Heaney repents a life that kept him 'competent / To sleepwalk with connivance and mistrust'. He yields to feelings of disgust in confessional self-abasement.

> I hate how quick I was to know my place.
> I hate where I was born, hate everything
> That made me biddable and unforthcoming.

But such vehemence goes against the grain of what he is. While he dramatises his hatred of all that made him what he is, he also accepts the way he is. The accusations end here; recovery comes in the abyss of guilt and self-blame. He has gained insight, sees, understands and is absolved. He discovers, or has confirmed, 'the need and chance / to salvage everything, to re-invisage'.

> I mouthed at my half-composed face
> In the shaving mirror, like somebody
> Drunk in the bathroom during a party,
> Lulled and repelled by his own reflection.
> As if the cairnstone could deny the cairn.
> As if the eddy could reform the pool.
> As if a stone whirled under a cascade,
> Eroded and eroding in its bed,
> Could grind itself down to a different core.
> Then I thought of the tribe whose dances never fail
> For they keep dancing till they sight the deer.

'As if' 'As if', 'As if' – there is no point to this sourfaced mood. 'There is nothing to confess' . . .

The poem ends in images of the dazzling cup, St. John of the Cross's absolving and confirming poem about love and beauty, the eternal fountain, full of light, unending, refreshing the world. 'No other thing can be so beautiful'. Joyce's admonitions confirm the importance of art and the poet's right to freedom.

Is the pilgrim-poet deeply riven? Even to speak of encounters, confrontations, or purgation is to use a language that seems too dramatic for most of what takes place. Heaney likes to make poems 'which are full of blessings and delights, which are celebrations, which in themselves are transformed, free things, which affirm that their one and only function is to be works which give delight'. But, at the same time, he was suspicious of giving pleasure. *Station Island*, he hoped, would redeem his right to write pleasurably.[3]

Both art and life bear upon the formation of the poet. In *Station Island* Heaney reveals his allegiance to both. The voices of the dead accuse him of connivance and evasion. Other voices urge him to steer clear of politics, to remember his duty as a poet. The poem shows that Heaney does not indulge complacently in lyric utterance while friends die and a people suffer. His is a 'voice that might continue, hold, dispel, appease'. He can clear his conscience through the pilgrimage, by showing himself torn, challenged, and responsive to suffering. He has the feeling and love that Hopkins identified as the true source of poetry. Through the pilgrimage, in its enactments of challenge and response, he purges his guilt. He can face the accusations, can mime the suffering, can present himself as sympathetically involved, can, in short, face the challenges and thereby earn the right to be free. He is both responsive and responsible. He feels the need to justify what he does, in particular the writing of free, lyric poetry, at a time and in a place where people suffer and are not free. He demonstrates that he does not run away from reality. That justifies the poem's conclusion. Poetry washes away the guilt and does so for all of us. It makes us, through the dramatic encounters, deeply aware of the very forces it transcends and transforms. We are unable to enjoy its lyric flight without being made deeply aware of the pain and the injustice. At the end of the journey Heaney arrives at a new level of consciousness. He has externalised his anxiety that in opting for poetry he failed his people, and has confirmed the redemptive power of poetry. We recognise honest self-questioning, reservations and tact in Yeats's 'Easter 1916'. We may recognise also the self-questioning, provisional assessments, renewed examination that go on throughout Heaney's poetry. He acts out what troubles him in a poetry of changing, subtle, dramatic self-revelation.

While the first part of *Station Island* contains poems of love and allegiance to familiar place and things, the last part, liberated through what the pilgrimage has achieved, flies into risk as the Joycean ghost advised. Sweeney flies high, runs free of the crowd, is not bound by kingdom or church, is pure artist writing his script. The figure of this Sweeney, already present in *Sweeney Astray* (1983), is an image of the self – away from the tribe, suffering separation and guilt, enjoying freedom. More ably and more complexly than we often realise Heaney plays the roles that are Sweeney-like, or rather uses Sweeney to accustom us to his own complex, unresolved situation. Part of our difficulty with Heaney is that he seems so familiar, so accessible, so able to assuage with his poetry, that we find it hard to be equally receptive to the complexity that troubles him. He does not seem to be a Hamlet, although he invokes him. He does not seem to be a Lear, although he frets upon the heath. He is more like Poor Tom, or the Fool, or Philoctetes with his wound and his bow in *The Cure at Troy* (1990), or Sweeney – comic in his cries and flutterings, tragically isolated in his treetop, the artist as victim, both insider and outsider. He ran free, 'mastered new rungs of the air', Ariel and Sweeney, to escape. Several of these poems are confident and self-contained affirmations of his freedom. We are accustomed to the mimetic artist up to the end of *North*,[4] less accustomed to the less self-conscious dramatising mode of the later books: 'he belongs to a tribe whose dances never fail'.

In *The Haw Lantern* (1987) and *Seeing Things* (1991), Heaney turns his attention in exact and exacting script to the alphabet of the original landscape. The haw lantern 'is a small light for small people', the only requirement 'that they keep / the wick of self-response from dying out, / not having to blind them with illumination'. As Diogenes searched for one just man, poetry looks keenly in judgement and the poet, too, would be tested. He lives in the republic of his own conscience, can write his own similitudes. When he passes into the clarified space the language only seems to be about actuality. It is, in fact, a risen language like the description of the chestnut tree once where he was, but now gone, 'Its heft and hush become a bright nowhere, / A soul ramifying and forever / Silent, beyond silence listened for'. Now he writes poetry of place with the materials of imagined spaces.[5]

In seeing things he may cross from one state of being to another. The familiar contains the preternatural. Poems find the marvellous in the ordinary, in spinning a bicycle wheel, in sliding, in the feints and aimings before shooting a marble, in letting go and coming back, as Aeneas did, enriched and strengthened. It is another kind of pilgrimage: to go 'Beyond our usual hold upon ourselves'.

Different versions of reality are brought side by side within individual poems and from one poem to its companion. The aim of the poetry is to cross thresholds, to be beyond and here, to hold contrasting images at once. The balance and poise of the pairings are a measure of the poet's own equilibrium. He sees what is there in the knowledge that 'whatever is given / Can always be re-imagined'. He is ready to 'credit marvels'. His injunctions are firmly grounded. 'Make your study the unregarded floor'. 'Sink every impulse like a bolt' . . . 'Do not waver / Into language. Do not waver in it'. The drama of self-measuring and revelation goes on. The pre-eminence of art over life is reaffirmed.

THE SWEET WAY

John Montague

Let us look at the historical implications of this meeting, summoned by our Muse, Jacqueline Genet. Six Irish writers are gathered in a French university to discuss that elusive thing called the creative process. That we are all of Catholic background, with no woman writer, may indicate that the bias Field Day stands accused of, in its anthology, is historical; there were very few Protestant or women writers in the period.

But there are notable changes. The two playwrights, the two Toms, work in a theatre far different from the Abbey of our youth. Playwrights are encouraged to write, to the point where even a poet could regard drama, as Yeats did, as part of the adventure. Our two novelists, the two Johns, can remember a time, especially McGahern, when writing a novel was a dangerous occupation, which might lead to job loss, ostracism and exile. What could they produce now which would have the sane seismic effect? From my own experience with the *novella*, *The Lost Notebook*, the audience, and the Censorship Board, are too cowed, or jaded to register righteous moral indignation.

As for the two poets, Seamus and myself, they do not have to fear either the loss of recognition which affected Clarke, or the lack of it which embittered Kavanagh. The Irish poetry scene is as lively as anything in the English speaking world, or beyond. Our peers are not elsewhere, like Auden and Berryman and Lowell, but our Irish contemporaries, Kinsella and Mahon: we have our own gold standard at home.

And invitations shower through the letter box, to Anglo-Irish literary conferences across the globe, Bloomsday festivities in Dublin Castle, first nights of Irish plays in London or New York. Literary work is not suspect, but highly rewarded, with Awards,

Bursaries, Travel Grants, the *cnuas*[1] of the Aosdana[2] to gratify the wolf at the door. Are they killing us with kindness so that we are unlikely to murmur dissent? Few Irish works deal with the present, but I do prefer the atmosphere of respect and care for the creative to the bowsy, brutal world in which I grew up, where you had to be the fastest word alive, to survive. Hype is our main enemy now, not sour neglect.

There is only one word to describe the way in which we were brought, or dragged up, that is barbaric. I am speaking of Dublin, of course, for there was very little in the North. One is often tempted to disguise, or soften, the clumsiness of one's upbringing, but Dublin in the late Forties and Fifties was a cactus-littered desert. Our English professor, Jeremiah Joseph Hogan, was *vox et preterea nihil*, a nullity who read out Milton in the artificial Oxford accent he had grafted onto his Dublin vowels. 'There are many fine things here,' he quavered to his cowed, bored audience, leaving me with no choice but to seek out the disloyal opposition in the pubs. But there was also the loyal opposition *intra muros*: a younger teacher called Roger MacHugh ran an evening course in Anglo-Irish Literature which in due course would become the Department in which two of our speakers work, Augustine Martin and Maurice Harmon. Joyce speaking in the Physics Theatre, Hopkins correcting Exam papers, Myles blathering in the Main Hall: the move to Belfield may have disturbed the literary tradition of U.C.D. but at least we now know it was there.

For the poet aspirant, things were equally depressing outside. Ireland's senior poet was Austin Clarke, whose *Collected Poems* were long out of print. Silver-haired with black hat and stick, he seemed elderly, defeated, although only in his early fifties, like Seamus Heaney here today. His radio programme on Radio Eireann was the only way Irish people heard of the Muse, after the Leaving Cert. He was also the main poetry reviewer for the *Irish Times*, thus dominating both approaches. Again, the opposition was more exciting, and demonstrated the historical importance of the move from the salon or *soirée*, essential to the Literary Revival, to the democratic, more Catholic atmosphere of the pub. Myles sunk in his *smahan*[1], Behan blustering through,

---

1. Stipend.
2. Society of Writers who receive an annual grant.

Sean O'Sullivan citing Baudelaire were all part of a stage set, an artistic happening which combined the horrible and the hilarious. But for the hard men, the rangy University wits, the key figure was Kavanagh, a hunched oracle delivering its own version of Arnold: 'has he the touch?'. Kinsella and I thought we had, but contemplating the Scylla of Clarke and the Charybdis of Kavanagh we were alarmed for our future.

A corrective for me was my dream of the French literary life. Cycling through post-war Paris, nineteen years old, with Rimbaud in my knapsack, I caught sight of the Cafe des Intellectuels, and felt a suitable frisson. I see a triple impulse at work here: I believed that there had to be an alternative to the savagery of Dublin pub life and where better than the city where our great exiles, Joyce and Beckett, had sought refuge? Besides, the impression of energy the French gave off, despite defeat, was a lift after Dublin and dingy London: the cafes of St. Germain were full.

Was that Sartre and Simone at a cafe table near the stove, papers spread wide? My still unpublished pal, Brendan Behan, claimed to have gone over to Jean-Paul at the Flore and introduced himself, saying, 'I'm a writer, too'. He also described marching with them all at Eluard's funeral. From long summer sessions in the Latin Quarter, Le Tabou, the Cabaret Vert, I think I inhaled the Existentialist doctrine of the creation of character by choice, a man as the sum of his/her actions. I studied Heidegger and *L'Etre et le Néant*, Mounier and Marcel, but it was the aphoristic exactness of the creative work of Camus and Sartre which drew me most: years later, I was delighted to find myself playing a small part in a film of *Le Mur*. Existentialism was an antidote to scholasticism, lay priests of the intellect, and the flesh; love and morality were not inimical but allied in the quest for self knowledge. And there was French poetry, the fluency of Eluard especially, a singing humanist, lover of liberty, lover of women. I would try to lead such a full, generous life as this prince poet of Paris, beloved friend of Picasso and the other painters.

It was not as easy as that: I was still gnawed by the Daedalus demon of ingrown self-consciousness. So I was impressed by the French *penchant* for the introspective, the *Journals* of Gide, and Cocteau, a fashionable figure, as poet, artist and film maker. And

------

1. His little drink.

the intense rhetoric of books like *Les Nouritures Terrestres* inflamed the flesh as well as the mind. The autobiographies of poets, Herbert Read, Edwin Muir, and above all Pierre Emmanuel's *Universal Singular*, which became a kind of Bible for me, a young Catholic celibate also seized by the poetic, with Austin Clarke as my version of the austere but sensual Jouve. One day, hopefully, I will manage an autobiography but when the truth will not harm, but instruct, as the senses slow towards wisdom, more Goethe than Gide, says he, presumptuously.

Crucial to the writing/reading of lyric poetry is our attitude towards love. The muse, surely, can be traced back to the paleolithic Earth Mother, the Laussel Venus who resembles so much our cruder Sheela-na-Gigs. This primitive awe before the creative power of the feminine was elevated and distanced into the doctrine of Courtly Love. Whether its origins are contaminated with patriarchal condescension, the urge to dominate by adoring, Western poetry, indeed most poetry, has acknowledged the religion of love as a central force, though I would argue for a wider definition of the Muse as whatever excites one to an awareness of the mystery, which for the Greeks was male beauty as well.

As a friend, and amused admirer of Robert Graves, and of the love poems of Yeats, I subscribe to this association between love and lyric, although it belongs to an area more of belief than proof. But in the East there is often a subtle difference; instead of the religion of love, which elevates the Lady, *la Donna* or the Blessed Virgin, we have love as a discipline, whether in the explicit details of Chinese prints, or the Tantric postures on the great Indian temples of Khajurao and Orissa. To achieve mystical states by diverting, instead of denying the flesh, may be a doctrine too strong for our colder climates. *Mithuna* , the mutually shared ecstasy of creative love, is a more practical form of erotic mysticism than *l'amour courtois*, and Paolo and Francesca would be more likely to find themselves in Heaven than Hell. Yeats glimpses it in his Ribh poems, and I have felt impelled to visit India thrice, to understand this Bower of Bliss. The room in the museum at Delhi where Shiva and Parvati, the male and female principles, interlace in their holy dance is a far step from the plaster virgins of my youth. But it is not far from the orgiastic glory which represents Paradise in early Irish, the Land of Women also known as The Honey Plain:

> Warm, sweet streams water the earth,
> And after the choicest of wine and mead,
> Those fine and flawless people
> Without sin, without guilt, couple.

The way to this Eden is through what the Irish call *An Cam Dilis*, the sweet path of love, older than de Sade or D.H. Lawrence, and far more enticing.

Then there is the mysterious loyalty to the older language: the majority of recent Irish poets have paid their tribute in translation, even with scant Irish. My first experience of it came from Father O'Devlin, later author of *The Parish of Donaghmore* which, with its high cross, was once part of our early church: Donaghmore, Arboe, and Errigal Keerogue suggest how deeply rooted it was in Tyrone. Then more extensively from Sean O'Boyle, whose extraordinary theories about Irish music and art were a preparation for later late night ruminations with Ó Riada.

Is there an Irish or Celtic aesthetic, older or at least different from the Classical, and reaching as far as Arabia and India? Climbing Loughcrew or Knockmany I can well believe it: I draw the double or triple spirals of those stones for an alchemist friend, and he identifies the uroboric vision of the serpent swallowing its own tail. On a personal level I notice that my two longer poems curve back to their beginnings, starting and ending with journeys.

Shapes are compounded of sounds and the Irish ear seems to me susceptible to quarter tones and grace notes. During the decade when I was assembling *The Rough Field* I was also involved in founding Claddagh Records, recording the best of the surviving musicians, like Denis Murphy from Sliabh Luachra, Maire Aine from Connemara, the most ancient sounds our country has produced. Playing *sean nos* in India the audience weave their heads to wavering rhythms that they seem to recognise. I no longer listen to that music with the same intensity but I am sure it influenced the structure of the emerging poem.

Whereas when I was working on *The Dead Kingdom* I played MacCormack records incessantly, recalling the voice of my own father raised in song, a man as intolerant as Simon Daedalus. Racism and bigotry are somehow allied to the tear and the smile in those heart-rending Irish melodies, which teeter on the edge of the sentimental. As Tom Murphy knows, inside an Irish writer there is often a tenor trying to get out.

Crucial is our cordial enmity/amity with England. Most of us write in English now, and are enamoured of the long tradition of the language, in which we were trained as scholars, and now use as a medium. Our historical unease may even make it more exciting to us. When I read the Elizabethans, I know that Raleigh was the duty officer at the Dingle massacre, and Spenser the recording clerk, on a break from elaborating *The Faerie Queene* in North Cork. In a few years the army of Tyrone would put an end to that ambition, as Mountjoy did to theirs, and Sir John Davies would help to orchestrate the change. It is as if Lowell and Berryman were at Mai Lai, with Robert Bly or Duncan waiting in the wings.

My own early admiration was for *Paradise Lost*, the masterwork of Cromwell's secretary, which I somehow connect with the Black North of my youth. I found Milton's slow choice of epic subject, as detailed by Tillyard, fascinating, and it perhaps influenced my deliberations in trying to locate a theme to draw out all my resources. Nowadays I feel closer to Wordsworth, and I am not alone in this. When I was examining the famous letter from Goslar in Dove Cottage, first draft of the skating scene in *The Prelude*, the curator came over to say that he had only seen one person regard the manuscript with such intensity, that he was from Ireland as well. No marks for guessing the Secret Sharer: he is sitting at this same forum.

Heaney and I have ruminated about the use of Hiberno-English: should he have said 'My father *wrought* with the horse plough?' Certain Ulsterisms are sanctioned by Shakespeare, it seems, but then he was a country boy as well. Our double-barrelled tradition affects not only details of language but modes as well. What in English is called topographical or pastoral deepens in Irish to *Dinnsheanchas*, or place wisdom; part of the equipment of the poet was in genealogy and local history. I find the same thing in writers from the other so-called Celtic countries, like MacDiarmid and Sorley MacLean from Scotland, and above all, David Jones in *The Anathemata*. His lovely, lonely sigh for the lost place names in 'The Tutelar of the Place' touches me to the quick, now that *The Rough Field* is known officially as *The Omagh Road*.

Finally let us consider the position of the poet in Irish society, or some such formula for the former *file*. The simple answer is that the poet has one, central or marginal, inside or outside, depending on the period. I am not venerable enough to remember when A.E., Yeats and the others walked the streets, although I did glimpse Maud Gonne, and knew George Yeats. Dublin was a small city, but its literary impact was enormous, for and against, since the literary exile has to have something to condemn or be condemned by, as Dante found with Florence. We have moved from the selectivity of the salon to the saloon or pub, but Kavanagh was a king in his quarter.

It may seem grandiose to trace this back to the position of the bard or *file* in feudal Gaelic society. But look at the other English speaking countries, especially America, where the poets take refuge in universities, like mediaeval sanctuaries. Lincoln met Whitman as a hospital orderly but he did not discuss poetry with him: meanwhile Emily Dickinson took to her room. Faint efforts have been made to draft the writer in America, like Kennedy with Frost, Carter and James Dickey, but when the Poet Laureate, Mark Strand, resigned recently he complained that he only met entertainers at the White House, Sinatra not Saul Bellow. And England is no better: Larkin seemed embarrassed by his gift, like Auden pretending he was something normal like a psychiatrist, when someone asked his profession.

Whereas we have a President who quotes poetry, and several Taoiseachs who have managed the odd line. In that mythical Dublin Four which is the Sunday Supplement version of the Fifth Province, poets are Philosopher Kings. Before leaving, I received several calls from a public relations firm, asking me, like most of the participants here, to some public event. Hearing the list, I asked what we all had in common and was told we were 'cultural notables'. Over-exposure is now the enemy but even when Kavanagh was lambasting his Ireland he was appealing to another, more lasting one. The lesson I still carry from the master poets of my youth is that poetry is the art of loneliness, as well as of praise, the spirit singing of the essential, with or against the tide. Or paradoxically both the art of loneliness, and an act of praise, the self singing to itself, free of the unessential, the dross.

JOHN MONTAGUE:
PASSIONATE CONTEMPLATIVE

Augustine Martin

The most terrible of the graffiti thrown up by the Catholic ghet-
toes of Northern Ireland over the past twenty-five years of
violence is also the most indigenous: 'Is there a life before death?'
Its dreadful aptness derives from the fact that it echoes the last
words of a prayer known intimately by every Catholic in the
region, the 'Salve Regina' or 'Hail Holy Queen'. Addressed to
Mary, Queen of Heaven, by her suppliants, 'poor banished children of Eve . . . mourning and weeping in this valley of tears' it
begs her, 'after this our exile', to show unto us, in Paradise, 'the
blessed fruit of thy womb, Jesus.' In reviewing *History Lessons*
almost a decade ago I was struck at how often the theme and
imagery of St Bernard's great hymn recurred in Seamus Deane's
vision of human existence in Derry:

> Real life was so impure
> We savoured its poisons as forbidden
> Fruit and, desolate with knowledge,
> Grew beyond redemption.

Elsewhere

> Someone is migrating.
> He is going to the fifth
> Season where he can hear
> The greenness planning its leaves.

And as if to prove its universality, in an invocation to Mandelstam
he calls on the 'Son of Petropolis' – keeper of heaven's gate? – to
teach us, exiles on the banks of the Styx, to wait

For the gossamer of Paradise
To spider in our dirt-filled eyes.

In re-reading the prose and poetry of John Montague I was
surprised, but not astonished, at the presence – under radically
different auspices – of the same motif and image. With him it is
most persistent in the love poetry where it is negotiated in terms
of myth or fiction, or transcending both modes, in his unique
commerce with the mystical. I will therefore concentrate not on
the political side of his work – which has received its share of
attention – but on his poetry of the heart's emotions, whether in
the form of *eros*, *agape*, *friendship* or *affection*.[1] No Irish poet has
explored these themes with such poignancy and toughness.[2]

When distinguishing the categories of myth, fiction and mysticism in Montague's work it's best to proceed by illustration
and epitome. 'The Wild Dog Rose', a meditation on Yeats's 'poor
foolish things that live a day', could hardly be further in its
human immediacy from the dreamy longing and complaint of
its precursor.[3] In one of Montague's earlier poems, 'Like Dolmens
Round my Childhood, the Old People', the poet felt haunted by
the strange old men and women of the parish – Jamie MacCrystal,
Maggie Owens, Mary Moore, Billy Harbison:

Gaunt figures of fear and of friendliness,
For years they trespassed on my dreams,
Until once, in a standing circle of stones,
I felt their shadows pass

Into that dark permanence of ancient forms.

Ten years later in 'The Wild Dog Rose' a different Montague
has retrieved at least one of them, the *cailleach* (Irish word for
hag), out of myth into the warmer individual idiom of fiction:

I go to say goodbye to the *cailleach*,
that terrible figure who haunted my childhood
but no longer harsh, a human being
merely, hurt by event.

They now can talk 'like old friends, lovers almost, / sharing
secrets' even to the extent that the old woman can confide to
him the one terrible adventure of her uneventful life. At the age
of seventy she has had her door broken in by a drunken farmer
intent on rape, with whom she struggles through the night. She

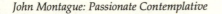
prays to 'the Blessed Virgin herself' and eventually breaks his
grip on her.

> He rolls
> to the floor, snores asleep,
> while she cowers until dawn
> and the dogs' whimpering starts
> him awake, to lurch back across
> the wet bog.

As she reflects the old woman observes that the wild dog
rose 'is the only rose without thorns' which reminds her of 'the
Holy Mother of God and / all she suffered'. The narrative has
passed from the intimate particularity of fiction into the fixity of
myth. The myth is in turn transcended in the poet's final meditation when briefly

> the air is strong with the smell
> of that weak flower, offering
> its crumbling yellow cup
> and pale bleeding lips
> fading to white
>   at the rim
> of each bruised and heart-
> shaped petal.

From the commonplace we have gradually moved upwards
through the mythical to the mystical, to the beatific vision of
Dante's multifoliate rose – 'and after this, our exile, show unto
us . . .' How close Montague identifies himself with this intensely
Catholic gesture of experience is tantalising and irrelevant. If
asked I suspect that he would smile and reply with Yeats: 'Homer
is my example and his unchristened heart'. What *is* relevant is
the mediation of the poet's multiple finesse in delivering the old
woman's transfiguring account of life before death.

Montague's most obsessive theme is erotic love, its glory, terror and mystery. His most dramatic exploration of the theme is
in his recent short fiction, *The Lost Notebook*,[4] which describes
with savage explicitness an affair between a callow Irish youth
visiting Italy for the Holy Year of 1950 – the 'Anno Santo' of an
earlier poem – and an American art student whom he meets and
lives with in Florence. The dogged imperfection of their love-
making as seen against the masterworks of art and symbols of

religion that make up the furniture of their life is powerfully
caught in the accompanying illustrations of John Verling. At the
story's end one senses amid the exertions of the flesh a sort of
frenzied search for the soul. But the mystery remains intact and,
at least for me, *The Lost Notebook* remains one of the great short
stories of our time. And its uncompromising ardour recalls to us
Montague's contemplation of that most obscene of Irish artefacts, Sheela na Gig.

These grotesque stone monuments, found here and there in
churchyards throughout the country, have puzzled scholars over
the centuries. What is their basic symbolism: a gross female shape
with its hands holding open the lips of the vagina? Is its meaning augmented or contradicted by its presence within the
monastic sanctuary? Is it a throwback from an older paganism
or a misogynist sermon in stone to foster male celibacy? What, if
anything, does it tell us about the Irish at prayer?

Montague uses the Sheela as frontispiece for his magisterial
1984 collection, *The Dead Kingdom*. *Eros* is not the volume's theme,
though it is related to the book's commerce with mutability and
death, natural process, sons and mothers, the dying generations.
Its dominant image is the salmon making its way upstream to
spawn, paralleled by the poet's journey northward through Ireland on hearing of his mother's death. It is a volume conducted
chiefly in the idiom of fiction, with vivid portraits of his rela-
tives, particular evocations of occasions and atmospheres. These
particularities are, however, deftly buttressed by a few formal
mythic statements, most notably 'Deities' and the stylish 'Invocation to the Guardian', but none of these bearing on the
symbolism of Sheela na Gig.

It is in *Mount Eagle* (1988), four years later and after the inter-
vention of *The Lost Notebook* that 'Montague confronts, with the
brutal impersonality of myth, the enigma of Sheela na Gig in a
poem of that name:

> The bloody tent-flap opens. We slide
> into life, slick with slime and blood.
> Cunt, or Cymric *cwm*, Chaucerian *quente*,
> the first home from which we are sent
> into banishment, to spend our whole life
> cruising to return, raising a puny mast
> to sail back into those moist lips
> that overhang *labia minora* and *clitoris*.

> To sigh and die upon the Mount of Venus,
> layer after layer of warm moss,
> to return to that first darkness!
> Small wonder she grins at us, from gable
> or church wall. For the howling babe
> life's warm start: man's question mark.

The poem's impact is complicated and enriched when we recall that the Christian monks who may have contemplated this sexual totem, shared in the doctrine of life as an *exilium* – 'the first home from which we are sent / into banishment – because of Eve's transgression; and in the allied belief that redemption would come through the mediation of the second Eve – Mary, Virgin and Mother. Then in the final phrase the generic 'babe' becomes male, adult, baffled by his eviction and exclusion. It is arguable that in Montague's erotic poetry the male is engaged in a perpetual quest for penetration and re-entry.

Either way the poem presents an emphatically modern consciousness perplexed before the aboriginal reality of sex, birth and motherhood, a vision that is ghosted perpetually by the Mariolatry through which he first apprehended these mysteries. 'Sheela na Gig' can be read, therefore, as Montague's one rude answer – conscious or unconscious – to the hyperdulia of the 'Salve Regina' with its caressing answer to the mystery of existence *sub specie aeternitatis*. But the matter has further complexities and other answers. As the writer is Montague, poet and story writer, these answers must be sought in diverse regions and under several species.

In an early poem of his, 'Auschwitz, Mon Amour', Montague exclaims; 'It takes a decade and a half, it seems, / Even to comprehend one's dreams'. A process of what Yeats called 'dreaming back' connects the poem 'Sheela na Gig' with the frontispiece of that suite of poems on mother, father and homeland, on rivers and spawning salmon, that make up *The Dead Kingdom*. 'Sheela na Gig' is the poet's mythic 'comprehending' of what he had fictionally perpetrated in *The Dead Kingdom* a mere four years earlier. That is his family book, his extended treatment of love under the species of *affection*. It follows upon his comprehensive testament to *eros* in the *The Great Cloak* (1978). Each volume has its answers to the overwhelming question posed in 'Sheela na Gig'. Let us go and make our visit first to *The Great Cloak*.

In the 'Plot' provided at the book's opening Montague ex-

plains the structure of its three sections. The first, 'Search', rehearses the extra-marital questings of a man whose marriage is
breaking down; the second, 'Separation', presents the 'despair-
ing voices' of that disintegrating relationship; the third, 'Anchor',
a 'new and growing relationship to which he pledges himself'.
The theme is of course continuous with those haunting love
poems of the first marriage with Madeleine which appeared in *A
Chosen Light* (1967), especially 'All Legendary Obstacles'; and the
three related lyrics of 'Loving Reflections' – one of them entitled
'Amo, ergo sum'. One may even identify a proleptic intimation
of Sheela na Gig in 'Loving Reflections' when in the midst of the
love act there occurs a 'Shudder of angels / Into grimacing stone'.

There are multiple levels of guilt in *The Great Cloak*. He begins his homage to *eros* by attempting to assuage Bellona:

> As my Province burns
> I sing of love,
> Hoping to give that fiery
> Wheel a shove.

There follows in 'Search' a sequence of love lyrics in which
the male persona, compunctious and predatory, moves from bed
to bed in service to

> the alluring lie
> of searching through another's pliant body
> for something missing in his separate self.

Though the sequence ends with the stylish if guilt-ridden swag-
ger of 'Don Juan's Farewell' there is an almost Augustinian
restlessness in the quest, an inescapable sense of exile from the
spiritual healing of love itself. And if the mysteries of *agape* are
well removed from the poet's aspiration, there is an undeniable
sense of paradise regained when his vision lifts from the furtive,
shadowy interiors of 'Search' to the sunlit Marian visions of the
Evelyn poems in the third section:

> Another day of dancing summer,
> Evelyn kneels on a rock, breasts
> swollen for approaching motherhood.
> Hair bleached by the sea winds
> To a pale as honey gold, some
> Generous natural image of the good.

In between, 'Separation' enacts the nightmare of estrangement. These dramatic lyrics are remarkable for their handling of
the primary emotions. Grief, loneliness, compunction, tenderness and rage find expression in a sort of frenzied duet, with the
persona neither of husband nor wife safely within earshot of the
other. The theme of childlessness recurs, sometimes in images of
gothic desolation, as when the abandoned wife, 'Habituée of
darkness', confronts her destiny in a dream:

> I came to where the eggs lay on the grass.
> I watched them for a long time, warming them
> With my swollen eyes. One after another
> The chipped and scraggy heads appeared:
> The embryos of our unborn children.
>
> They turn towards me, croaking 'Mother'.

Thus through a sequence of scary nocturnes Montague rehearses
the ordeals of estrangement to their culmination in 'Herbert Street
Revisited', where he lays the memories of their early love among
the homely ghosts of Behan, Nurse Mullen and Molly Malone:

> To summon back the past,
> and celebrate a love that eased
> so kindly, the dying bone,
> enabling the spirit to sing
> of old happiness, when alone.

The poems of 'Separation' are among the most powerful in
Montague's work. They are emphatically poems of spiritual exile in which the poet insists upon exposing the intensity of a love
experience that survives only in its stubborn, prehensile pain.
When we sense their continuity with the earlier Madeleine love
poems of *A Chosen Light* it is because their feel is the same, a
feel uniquely and intensely modern, of lovers insisting on the
sufficiency of their two selves, reaching out for all the attendant
risks. The hero is an adult version of the male who has been
tested in the fires of *The Lost Notebook*, released from his Irish
Catholic inhibitions, exorbitant in his demands upon the beloved,
and upon their shared existential flesh and blood. The ecstasy
of 'All Legendary Obstacles' set against the violence of 'The
Blow' had already set up the coordinates by which the angst of
'Search' and 'Separation' seem more than consequential, almost
inevitable.

'Anchor' as already noted is all sunshine, sea, sky, and tranquillity. Odysseus, sea-wracked and world-weary has found landfall and safe haven 'in the harbour's arms'. The profane images, both pagan and existential, for the moment withdraw. Nausicaa becomes real as wife and mother in the person of Evelyn, radiantly at home on the coast of Cork:

> Edenlike as your name
> this sea's edge garden
> where we rest . . .[5]

In a sense it is the 'simplicity of return' which Kavanagh had declared the 'ultimate of sophistication'. The sequence is alive with celebration, images of redemption, a terminology of light, grace and prayer.

> Or when the baby is born
> to wrap the morsel tenderly
> while beasts browse around them
> naturally as in Bethlehem.

The stony horror of Sheela na Gig is confronted and down-faced in the natural miracle, the 'blood kin of birth':

> Awed, I bent in my gauze mask
> to stroke your trembling hands
> While our daughter was hauled
> and forced into this breathing world.

This moment of fulfilment, tenderness and rest is Montague's first real exploration of love under the species of affection. It is from here that the reverie over his own nativity, and the uncertainty of his setting forth, begins to gather, and to shape the context of *The Dead Kingdom*.

This volume opens dramatically and sustains its long drama of self-discovery with that uncanny, fictive sense of the particular that Montague brings to the human details of his imagined landscape. With the news of his mother's death: he notes

> the strangeness of Evelyn
> weeping for someone
> she had never known

while he stands dry-eyed

> phoning and phoning a cousin
> until, cursing, I turn
> to feel his shadow loom
> across the threshold.

Moments as psychologically real and impeccably timed as this underpin the complicated world of family that the reader finds himself entering, an unfolding web of history, incident, symbol, metaphor and myth. The cousins drive northward across the sleepy plains of the Republic – the 'neutral realm' which gives its name to the book's second section – towards Ulster, the tragic province of the poet's ancestors. Sensing a mysterious homing instinct the poet likens them to the salmon leaping upstream to find its immemorial breeding-ground.

> Secret, lonely messages
> along the air, older than
> humming telephone wires,
> blood talk, neglected
> affinities of family,
> antennae of instinct
> reaching through space,
> first intelligence.

They enter a region of myth as they cross The Black Pig's Dyke – Yeats's Valley of the Black Pig – that marks the border of Ulster. This region, in Irish prophecy the site of Armageddon, reveals a 'sand-bagged barracks', overture to contemporary warfare. An irruption of intimate rage – more personal than anything in *The Rough Field* (1972), gives a new dimension to Montague's meditations on history when he turns on the wrong of 'imperial policy'[6]

> Hurling the small peoples
> against each other, Orange
> Order against defender
> neighbour against neighbour,
> blind rituals of violence,
> our homely Ulster swollen
> to a Plain of Blood.

The word 'homely', hinting at a new possessiveness towards Tyrone, his territory – characterised in *The Rough Field*, as a 'by-passed and dying place' – signals the sense of that radical home-coming that is the book's overriding concern. The travellers negotiate their way through a forest of myths – Norse maledictions, Red Branch blessings, Christian saints, the deities of Ireland, India and Greece, as they approach home and the last two sections of the book, 'The Silver Flask' and 'A Flowering Absence' where myth yields, almost completely, to the more domestic intimacies of fiction.

I began this meditation by suggesting that the sense of spiritual exile expressed in the 'Salve Regina' is to be found in the imagery of poets brought up in the Irish Catholic tradition. It is important to register here that the phrase 'poor banished children of Eve' might have had special and poignant significance for the poet who wrote the last poems of *The Dead Kingdom*. These confessional lyrics unfold piecemeal, almost with reluctance, the painful history of a child born in Brooklyn into the Depression of 1929. His vivacious mother, Molly Carney, had come to America with her two eldest sons to join her husband, only to find him demoralised by unemployment and drink. In 1936 she took her sons back to the 'familiar womb-warm basket' of her Carney home at Fintona. The poem which recounts it all, 'A Muddy Cup', ends with a twist of uncharacteristic bitterness as the reductive animal imagery is intensified:

> (all but the runt,
> the littlest one, whom
> she gave to be fostered
> in Garvaghy, seven miles away:
> her husband's old home).

The awfulness of this rejection – shrewdly rendered in the grammar of parenthesis – is considerably assuaged by the love lavished on the boy by his two Montague aunts, acknowledged with tact and tenderness both in 'A Flowering Absence' and in 'Postmistress; a Diptych' from his latest volume, *Mount Eagle*. But the grief is pursued relentlessly through this suite of poems as he seeks to 'manage the pain – how a mother gave away her son'. His own experience of parenthood has given a new edge both to the pain and the mystery:

> There is an absence, real as presence.
> In the mornings I hear my daughter
> chuckle, with runs of sudden joy.
> Hurt, she rushes to her mother,
> as I never could, a whining boy.

A kind of answer comes in 'The Locket' where he recalls that he cycled to Fintona to win back his mother in a strange ritual of courtship, only to be told not to come again – 'I start to get fond of you, John, / and then you are up and gone'. The mature poet, who has trafficked more widely, though perhaps not as deep, in rejection, estrangement and disappointment, begins to apprehend the mystery he had set himself to understand:

> And still, mysterious blessing,
> I never knew, until you were gone,
> that, always around your neck,
> you wore an oval locket
> with an old picture in it,
> of a child in Brooklyn.

Is it significant that the blessing is followed by another religious trope, the 'New Litany' as *The Dead Kingdom* comes to a close? It is in fact a prayer for his mother's repose as he sees her best parts reincarnated in his wife, Evelyn, whose name he did not dare mention to the dying woman when she inquired for Madeleine from her death bed. The litany itself comprises the place-names of an adopted habitat, names mostly Christian – Roche's Point, Brandon, Gabriel, Sybil Head – but shrewdly pagan and occult in their ministry to the poetic soul:

> powers made manifest,
> amulets against loneliness,
> talismans for works:
> a flowering presence?

His father, James Montague, bears at once a substantial yet shadowy role in the web of circumstance that makes up the drama of *eros* and *affection* that culminates in *The Dead Kingdom*. (*Friendship* is a sporadic concern in Montague's work, though memorably expressed in his 'Ballad for Berryman' and his tribute to a Protestant neighbour, Billy Davison in 'A Real Irishman', both in the later *Mount Eagle. Agape,* in some trepidation, I leave to last.) It must be significant that James Montague began to appear in *The Rough Field* (1972) long before the poet could confront the emotional challenge of his mother's memory. Poems like 'Stele for a Northern Republican', 'The Cage' and 'The Fault' had already established an unforced empathy with this flawed, feckless but affectionate parent who had persisted with an aimless life in Brooklyn after his family had returned to Ireland.

In *The Dead Kingdom* his history is completed in four vivid sketches: 'A Christmas Card' which imagines the old man's lonely existence in Brooklyn; 'At Last' when John and his two brothers meet him as he disembarks from the boat at Cobh and drive him home across Ireland; in 'The Silver Flask' where the reunited family motor to Midnight Mass and, on the way home, pass round the hip-flask of whiskey – counter-image to the muddy cup which the mother had refused to taste in Brooklyn; in 'Last Journey' where he is more a memory, an unflowering absence, than a presence on the train out of Fintona. It is perhaps typical of the culture that the father, unlike the mother, is hardly called to account for his absence and neglect. Like the elder Dedalus he had natural friendliness – and a ready tenor voice in which he had found time to 'croon to his last son'. The brush-strokes of characterisation bring him poignantly to life:

> A small man with a hat
> he came through the customs at Cobh
> carrying a roped suitcase and
> something within me began to contract . . .

at Mass

> My father joining warmly in,
> his broken tenor faltering,
> a legend in dim bars in Brooklyn . . .

> Startling the stiff congregation
> with fierce blasts of song, while
> our mother sat silent beside him
> sad but proud . . .

The Dead Kingdom ends with a poem called 'Back' in which the burial is over, and the two cousins make the return journey southward with 'goodbyes decently said' and 'honour satisfied'. In so many ways the complexities of wandering and exile have been resolved. The last word in the book is 'home'.

I have been arguing that John Montague's poetry is overwhelmingly a meditation upon 'love's bitter mystery', that *Amo, ergo sum* might justly be his motto. Erotic and family affection are at the centre of his poetic focus, and these two themes are intimately related, finding their most eloquent expression in *The Great Cloak* and *The Dead Kingdom*. His complex and varied exploration of these massive themes is characterised by a profound, but not necessarily conscious, sense of life as a state of exile; and the imagery through which this insight is expressed may have been absorbed with the prayers and teachings of a Catholic childhood. These perceptions found unique confirmation in the circumstances of his own life story. His poetry is the most intense, honest, varied and accomplished expression of 'love's bitter mystery' among Irish poets since Yeats, and has few rivals in the whole range of contemporary writing.

The question of transcendence, mysticism, *agape*, remains. It is the hardest region of art to explore because its tendency is to discard the embodying agencies of myth and fiction in its pursuit of the inexpressible. Montague's mysticism, his search for the transcendent, derives, I suspect, as much from Hinduism as from any Christian source. His visits to India and his delighted reading of the *Vedas* and the *Book of Gilgamesh* – quoted at length in *The Dead Kingdom* – may contribute to a sense of the flesh as a pathway to the spirit that one senses in much of his love poetry.

These 'bright shoots of everlastingness' pervade that neglected volume, *A Chosen Light* (1967), even when the theme is not overtly sexual. The volume takes its title from a moment of intense contemplation in the dawn of a Paris garden:

> In that stillness – soft but luminously exact,
> A chosen light – I notice
> The tips of the lately grafted cherry tree.

The miracle of the graft, of art enhancing nature, is perceived in an unearthly moment, and the light of eternity. More often that sense of transcendence occurs in the silence created by a poem's ending. At the end of 'The Trout' the poet's sense of the numinous is left tingling on the air: 'To this day I can / Taste its terror on my hands'.

'All Legendary Obstacles' is Montague's supreme example of a love poem in this metaphysical mode. Artfully placed in that volume opposite 'Sentence for Konarak' which celebrates the spiritual end of the temple dancer's ritual of love, it enacts a ritual of longing. In the first three stanzas all of Montague's fictional skills are summoned to create the poet's long, nervous wait at the Californian railway station for his beloved's train to come:

> You had been travelling for days
> With an old lady, who marked
> A neat circle on the glass
> With her glove, to watch us
> Move into the wet darkness
> Kissing, still unable to speak.

In those earlier poems this mood and aura takes us by surprise. A sort of ambush from the quotidian, it leaves us with a sense of another and greater reality beyond the language and the occasion. In the more recent *Mount Eagle*, however, the approach is more formal, more metaphysical in both senses of the word. Poems like 'Crossing', 'The Leap', 'Hill of Silence', 'Gabriel' and 'The Well-Beloved' produce the urgent sense of a reality beyond the material world. The evidence for this other world resides in the poetic impulse which keeps insisting on it, and the sexual impulse whose ministry it is 'to transform the night / with love's necessary shafts of light'.

'The Hill of Silence', second last poem in the volume, has a long ancestry in Eastern religion and in Irish Christian tradition. The ascent, whether mystical or penitential, towards the summit, can symbolise an approach to God or the oversoul, to beatitude or nirvana. It can be an acknowledgement of earthly imperfection, heavenly glory. In more secular terms it may mean the quest for the perfection that is art. In the poem's ambiguous litany it embodies the physical and spiritual with the moral as it is called 'the slope of loneliness', 'the hill of silence', 'the wind's fortress', 'Our world's polestar', a 'stony patience'. The poetic voice, negotiating in the first person plural, takes us upwards in a priest-like *Levate*, through seven movements (the 'Seven Storied Mountain', the seven levels of karma, the seventh heaven of Islam?). The final phase, which I quote in full, suggests a mystical homecoming, an end of exile, if not indeed a vision of Paradise itself, as in the last line 'the animals gather round'.

> Let us lay ourselves
> down in this silence
>
> let us also be healed
> wounds closed, senses cleansed
>
> as over our bowed heads
> the mad larks multiply

needless stabbing the sky
in an ecstasy of stitching fury

against the blue void
while from clump and tuft

cranny and cleft, soft footed
curious, the animals gather round.

II.

THE IRISH PLAYWRIGHTS
AND THE CREATIVE PROCESS

FROM PAGE TO STAGE

Thomas Kilroy

I am going to jump about a bit but I hope to remain in the one territory, that area between writing on the page and performance upon a stage, a dimension in which one kind of creative activity is translated into another, where writing becomes action. Because I write prose fiction as well as plays and because I'm writing a novel at present I'm also going to try to say something about these two different kinds of writing. That discussion, too, belongs in the same territory or, at least, the territory offers a vocabulary to the discussion, a vocabulary of contrasts.

It is the contrast between the room and the stage, between the sedentary activity at the desk and the highly physical activity on the rehearsal floor. Since the act of writing includes within it the act of reading (so much writing depends upon rereading) writing, whether we like to acknowledge it or not, is conditioned by the way in which the writer perceives its eventual reception. A writer creates his readers, a playwright his audience. So, one contrast between novel-writing and playwriting is that between the psychology of the private reader and the psychology of an audience.

Finally, by way of general introduction, I've been thinking about the one feature of playwriting which would appear to run counter to the very principle of literary method which is generally accepted as resting upon the strict control of a single authority. No other aspect of playwriting bewilders other writers as much as the playwright's apparent surrender of creativity to a third party, to the community of people who stage the play, actors, designers, directors and so forth. Playwrights, of course, don't see this as a surrender at all. A play on the page is an appeal to be acted, to be staged. And a play is only readable when the reader is able to supply this amplification of the text, in effect, imaginatively supplying a theatre of the mind.

To shift gears, then, from the writing of plays to the writing of novels is to move from writing which resounds within a sounding chamber to one which flowers in silence and privacy, the creative silence of the reader that Sartre spoke of. The shift is radical, involving differences in the demands upon language, in the mode of character representation and in the timing, the pacing of narrative. We're talking about two different kinds of artifice.

The eighteenth century Japanese master of puppet plays, Chikamatsu, once said: 'Art is something which lies in the slender margin between the real and the unreal – it is unreal and yet it is not unreal. It is real and yet it is not real. Entertainment', he concluded, 'that is, the pleasure to be had from art – lies between the two'.

To illustrate his point he told a story of a great lady of the court who was separated from her lover, confined, as she was, deep within the confines of the women's palace. She could only peep at him through the slats of intervening screens. So great was her longing for him that she had a puppet made, life-size and an exact replica of her lover. It was made with such ingenuity that the pores of his skin were visible, each tooth was in place. When the lady received this doll its versimilitude, the perfection of its representation, chilled her body and eventually led to a deep disgust. She threw it away.

The story, of course, is about puppetry and the degree of stylization that should or should not be in the making of a puppet. And it may also have a peculiar resonance for the distancing effect in Japanese Noh and Bunraku theatre. But as writers we are all puppeteers. As writers we manipulate for effect. It is simply a question of how we hide our hands. It is an affectation, periodically indulged in, to say that the artist is a wholly natural phenomenon, a divine monster of nature, uncontaminated by intention. As someone once put it, the words of a poem come out of a head, not out of a hat.

In the sixties, as many of you will remember, there was a great debate about the importance of a writer's intention in the composition of a work and whether or not such an intention was important to the person reading the page or to the audience sitting in a theatre watching the play in performance. The Intentional Fallacy, the title of a famous essay of the day, was much bandied about. Everywhere there was heated discussion about

Interpretation. In particular it was asked to what extent has the individual play or poem or novel to stand alone? To what extent is it a discrete artefact? Well, the answer to that, like the answer to most things in life, is that it is and it isn't.

It's not so much that a writer begins with intention. It is that intention is subjected, along with the rest of the baggage, to the process, the flux. What begins as one thing can end up as something entirely different.

Some years ago I was trying to write a play about the beating up of a prostitute, a woman. It was based on a story that had been told to me, of this unfortunate person staggering around Rathmines, badly beaten after a gang-bang by a group of men in a flat. I found this story peculiarly gripping. It seemed to be saying something to me about the sexual violence of the Dublin I knew in the fifties, especially the Dublin of the flats, that place of frying-pans and bottled stout, of bicycle lamps and fumbling encounters between the sexes on Saturday nights. The point is that I spent a long time trying to write that play but it resisted me. There seemed to be something flabby at its centre, a lack of hard edge. I had my intention, certainly, but it seemed to be going nowhere. Then, quite suddenly and why I don't know, the woman became a male homosexual and the play wrote itself in a couple of weeks. The play, *The Death and Resurrection of Mr. Roche*, is not, of course, a play about homosexuality. It is a play about men in the absence of women. But I needed to take a side-step in order to go in a straight line.

What I'm trying to do here is underline the artifice of the writing enterprise and maybe come a little closer to that 'slender margin' of Chikamatsu and how it may be inhabited by invented figures. All fiction, to one degree or another, is autobiographical with the facts changed. I think it is drawn from what might be called the shaped biography of the writer, an internal biography which is emotional, psychic and may be quite unrepresented by the factuality of the lived life. This is what makes the matching of fiction and factual biography such a hazardous business. I would go further and say that the more vital the work the more it is infused with a specific personality, what Henry James once called 'the quality of mind of the producer'. The changing of the facts is what is mysterious and at its best it seems to happen in a kind of ruthless indifference to what is, in order to serve what might be. Maybe this helps to account for one of the great paradoxes in the history of art: how persons who are capable of monstrous behaviour are also capable of creating sublime beauty upon the page or stage.

In so many ways the kind of things which stimulate a writer into writing do not correspond to the kind of journey which the writer is trying to make in daily life. While we are about it we should also acknowledge that, because writers are themselves voracious readers, the autobiographical, in the sense that I've been using the word, always includes the writings of others. The bag of Autolycus is part of a writer's equipment. To paraphrase John Updike, we read in order to see what we can steal. At the heart of the enterprise, then, is a sort of cultural plunder, a busy burial, a furtive seeding and reseeding, a dedication to deception worthy of a criminal but also a splendid rising to disregard of all given conditions in this life and a huge need to put in place an alternative construction.

A thing of artifice, then, written down, destined to have its full expression on that page or destined to be lifted off the page and given its full expression upon the stage. The implication is that one text is somehow finished and the other not. But this would be to miss the point that a play has enfolded within it its full stage potential. Its theatricality is already written into it and I'm not talking about stage directions and the like. In a kind of ascription, the words of a play invite representation and this is because, in the writing, a playwright is not merely realising a character but is also hearing an actor performing that character at the same time. Without this dual, simultaneous function in the writing a play will be lifeless upon the stage. Stage figures are stage figures because they have been conceived from the beginning in terms of performance.

On the other hand, however allusive the style may be, the writer of prose fiction has sealed the language and experience on the printed page. Without considerable adaptation, there is simply no space there for the interpretative skills of the actor or director. Some writers of prose fiction, it is true, have a higher histrionic quality than others. In Irish writing where the capacity for self-dramatization is ingrained in the culture, you get this more than in most other bodies of literature. Orality is theatrical. But this is a secondary feature of this writing, a kind of mannerism.

I now want to turn to two specific aspects of writing for the stage. You could describe them as forms of restrictiveness since they refer to the peculiar intensification of theatre, the way it narrows down experience demanding a similar focus in the writing. I am going to talk about these because they have posed particular problems to me and I believe the essential problem has been that I have tried to import technique which, perhaps, might more properly be used in prose fiction.

The first is that plays are often written at great speed. There is even a school of thought which claims that in order to work, a play has to be written in this one hot blast. It is as if the tempo on stage, highly concentrated and driving, has to be mimicked in the act of writing itself. As I've already indicated, once the shape became clear, this is how my own play *The Death and Resurrection of Mr. Roche* was written. But I rarely work like this.

Let me give two very well known examples from contemporary theatre of the kind of thing I am talking about.

In his appalling book, *A Better Class of Person*, John Osborne offers us entries from his pocket diary as follows: '4th May, 1955. Began writing *Look Back in Anger*. Friday May 6th, *Look Back in Anger*, Act I, finished. 17th May – Act II sc. I, finished. Friday 27th May – *Look Back in Anger*, Act II finished. Friday, June 3rd *L.B. in A*. – finished.'

In his book *Timebends* Arthur Miller describes a very similar experience with the writing of *Death of a Salesman*. It is prefaced by a curious ritual where Miller, under some weird compulsion, is driven to build a shack, by hand, in the woods where he is to do the writing of the play. What follows is a kind of manic spasm. When he started, in April 1948, he had but two ingredients, the opening two lines of the play and the knowledge that there would be a death within the plot.

I started writing one morning – I worked all day until dark and then I had dinner and went back and wrote until some hours in the darkness between midnight and four. I had skipped a few areas that I knew would give me no trouble in the writing and gone for the parts that had to be muscled into position. By the next morning I had done the first half, the first act of two. When I lay down to sleep I realised I had been weeping – my eyes still burned and my throat was sore from talking it all out and shouting and laughing. I would be stiff when I woke, aching as if I had played four hours of football or tennis and now I had to face the start of another game. It would take six more weeks to complete Act II.

What Miller offers in addition, and Osborne doesn't, is the gestation behind this hot writing, the rag-bag collecting of this and that, the prowling around the material, half in fear that there might be no way in, the mixture of chance and opportunism which leads to the sharp point of knowledge, of knowing this thing in a kind of totality so that it can be written down in a frenzy for fear that it might be lost. Among the odds and ends for Miller was the discovery of the name Loman in Fritz Lang's film *The Testament of Dr. Mabuse* and the effect upon him of the first production in New Haven of Tennessee Williams' play *A Streetcar Named Desire*. For Miller, Williams had given American writing the licence to express feeling at a high pitch upon the stage.

There are many playwrights who can testify to the kind of experience recounted by Miller, the tears and talking and shouting and all. Plays that are fuelled by a single motor are more likely to benefit from this type of fierce winding up of energy and its explosive release. There is no doubt about the kind of power which it can muster on stage. My own problem is that I am, as a writer, more interested in the multi-layered play, the play which tries to hold several planes of action in place at the same time. I have to say that my interest in this kind of play comes from my interest in prose fiction where this layered structure is commonplace.

To turn to something different now, the second form of restrictiveness that I want to talk about in the theatre: the physical confines of the stage itself or acting space. I've written elsewhere that playwrights write plays in order to populate an empty space. I mean this in a literal sense. For a playwright, there is no place as moving, as imaginatively exciting, as an empty stage. There is also no place more desolate. It is an intense model of all desert places unwarmed by human presence. This intensity, however, is not of nature but of artifice, a platform of 'split deal' in Ben Jonson's phrase, that becomes animated through the eye of the voyeur, the ear of the eavesdropper, the expectant imagination of an audience.

Somewhere within this nexus is the dynamic of playwriting and it is removed from where most other literary works are plotted and executed. Dramatic technique is anything which serves to excite the expectation of an audience and then proceeds to satisfy it. It is inextricably bound up with a physical space, a place where it is to be made to happen and this stage-sense has to be present at all times in the writing of a play. At its crudest it must be there so that the playwright may efficiently move about the figures and the furniture, at its most profound it intensifies human behaviour.

This is the 'slender margin' of Chikamatsu which has the property of intensifying, of condensing human action in a way that might appear ludicrous or intolerable outside its confines. It is for this reason that some plays read so badly, appear to be so badly written when read according to external standards, external, that is to the mystery box of the stage where they have complete credibility. To the merely literary ear their rhetoric is too inflated, their conception of character carries too large a shadow to be believable. To speak about such writing clearly requires a different set of terms to that which we apply to a lyric poem or a piece of prose fiction.

As a playwright I think I've been carrying on a resistance to the limiting effects of stage space and in particular to the limited tolerance which the physical nature of theatre imposes upon an audience. I've spent some time, sometimes with unhappy results, in trying to test that tolerance, again, largely because I have tried to experiment with material which doesn't sit easily within a stage play. Again, I feel that this tendency comes from the way in which my mind has been conditioned by prose fiction.

Some months ago I started to write a voice. At first I thought it might be a voice in a play. But then the voice began to create a context around itself which could never be accommodated within a dramatic monologue. This needed the rhythm of silent reading if it were to work. There were no spaces here for actorly interpretation and the developing looseness of incident meant that it couldn't be contained upon the stage.

I want to end by reading a page from this fictional voice. The voice is that of a pedantic, fastidious bank clerk called Quirke who lives in a small town, married to an independently wealthy woman. He is a man given to hallucination which comes from a crisis that he is undergoing during the computerization of his branch of the bank. Physical surfaces disintegrate before his eyes but in the process he is given access to hidden mysteries.

Here is Quirke in his garden.

I was in the garden with Reilly the help propped up on his spade. There was an ancient prunus nearby and Stitch the dog sat at a distance, observing all, the very picture of malice.

'That's a whore of a bush', Reilly spat at the leaves. 'The more you cut off her the worse she gets'.

I bent to look as to an invitation. What a fool! The corrugated bark appeared to be giving off a slight sweating about its scabs. This was quickly followed by a pulsating and straining of the knobbly surface like a vegetative laying or hatching or letting of an inflammation. Stupidly I leant nearer still.

Before I could jump clear I was propelled with great force into a woodedness. I can only describe it as a shute or suction or maybe a press or heave which hurtled me in and through this element. The thing was surprisingly porous while still having this fibrous consistency of timber. But what was shocking beyond anything I had ever experienced in my life was the velocity with which I sped and the immense heat that went with it. Obviously I was shedding all human frailty as I tore through this fiery membrane, otherwise how could I have endured such speed, such heat? The clue, I believe, to this remarkable insulation of mine was that as I sped I became smaller and smaller. By the time I reached the node I was next to nothing.

'Hauld up yer head there's a good man', Reilly yelled. 'You're only after taken a turn you misfortunate. You'll be right as rain in a couple of minutes'.

Why was he yelling? Was there some evidence that I had gone deaf? He gripped my shoulders with those great hands of clay. Staggering about, the two of us, over a wheelbarrow, I made him promise not to tell anyone of what had happened to me in the garden. He put on that long pious Irish face of his which assured me that he would tell every Tom, Dick and Harry about how your man had fallen into the bush.

When I got back into the house I reported to the wife.

'I had a vision in the garden', I told her, limply.

'You had a what? What on earth are you going on about, Dodo?'

I was unable to give her any details that would have relieved the ridiculous simplicity of that first statement though, as you will have observed, I would have been perfectly capable of so doing whatever it was that stopped me.

THOMAS KILROY'S WORLD ELSEWHERE

Christopher Murray

What I shall attempt in this essay is the provision of a specific but ramifying set of contexts within which the plays of Thomas Kilroy may be examined and understood. In one way the work itself provides a context: it is constantly developing, constantly changing, and the latest play is probably best measured in relation to the earliest. So, for the most part, the critics who have written on Kilroy's work tend to argue.[1] But there is also a broad, general context into which Kilroy, a very self-aware writer, may more fruitfully be placed: the context of modernism. This is the one on which I want to concentrate.

Modernism contains several strands which have to be distinguished here. By modernism is meant that movement in literary history dating from the end of the nineteenth century which demarcated the old world from the new:

Indeed Modernism would seem to be the point at which the idea of the radical and innovating arts, the experimental, technical, aesthetic ideal that had been growing forward from Romanticism, reaches formal crisis – in which myth, structure and organization in a traditional sense collapse, and not only for formal reasons. The crisis is a crisis of culture.[2]

The editors of *Modernism 1890-1930* go on to describe it as the expression of a massive shift in consciousness, responding to 'the scenario of our chaos' and depicting the breakdown of traditional modes of perceiving and relating to experience:

It is the art consequent on the disestablishing of communal reality and conventional notions of causality, on the destruction of traditional notions of the wholeness of individual character, on the linguistic chaos that ensues when public notions of language have been discredited and when all realities have become subjective fictions. Modernism is then the art of modernization.[3]

So far as the drama is concerned, modernism begins with the revolutionary work of Ibsen, Strindberg and Chekhov, who between them altered the whole paradigm of theatre in its relationship to life, the whole concept of *mimesis*. For the sake of clarity I'm confining my argument here to the example of Ibsen, the Ibsen, shall we say, of André Antoine and the *Théâtre Libre*.[4]

Modern drama since Ibsen seems largely to be based on the tension, the dialectic, between an imitation of the world and a more disturbing actuality. Ibsen's first social dramas, *The Pillars of Society* (1877) and *A Doll's House* (1879), for example, present a picture of routine, middle-class life which masks a reality compounded of horror and lies. The world of outer solidity and ordinariness is revealed to be but a mask for a nightmarish truth. The action of an Ibsen play takes the form of an ironic exposure of a world elsewhere. When this other world is brought to the imagination, when the audience can apprehend the utter corruption of Consul Bernick's very soul and of Torvald Helmer's total self-interest, the trappings that gave such authenticity to the setting stand as so much disguise to the naked truth. The function of modern drama is here defined. The image of that function is graphically supplied in Ibsen's *Peer Gynt* (1867) when Peer peels the rinds of the onion until nothing is left and he knows he has met the hollowness of his own soul. Thus audiences are brought to see a void which they would perhaps prefer to ignore and this confrontation demands a response: at the least an assent, at best an appalled recognition and perhaps an expansion of consciousness.

A lot of Irish drama since 1899 is built upon Ibsen, whether directly or indirectly. Edward Martyn, one of the founding fathers of the Irish Literary Theatre, predecessor of the Abbey, deliberately co-opted Ibsen's style of drama as his own. *The Heather Field* (1899), *Maeve* (1900) and *The Tale of a Town* (1900) (the latter rewritten by another Ibsenist, George Moore), bear witness to this fact. Kick against Ibsen though he did, Yeats for his part could not turn back the tide in his influence. Shaw, Joyce, Colum, Synge and Lennox Robinson all in turn made use of the Ibsenist stage, the double agenda of his naturalism. Yeats went his own way, destabilizing the stage setting, presenting a symbolic basis for a drama taking place in what he called 'the deeps of the mind'.[5] And yet what he was trying to do actually resembled Ibsen's programme of revelation. As he said, 'we had the same enemies',[6] by which he meant materialism and its bourgeois producers. This resemblance is most clearly seen in the Yeatsian plays which make iconic use of naturalistic detail, in *The Land of Heart's Desire* (1894), *Cathleen Ni Houlihan* (1902), *Words upon the Window-Pane* (1930) and *Purgatory* (1938). In these plays to say that there is a rejection of the material world in favour of a spiritual world would be too crude and too easy a formulation. But it is undoubtedly the case that the Young Man in *Cathleen* rejects the clothes and the money which are the emblems of his binding to a new bride and to bourgeois responsibilities, and he forsakes the three-dimensional cottage for the open space that leads out to the war-like voices initiating the rising of 1798. It is possible to poke fun at Yeats's dialectic, or to condemn it as politically naive, since it endorses blood sacrifice; but it is not possible to deny that the action of that play, as of so many of Yeats's plays, turns on the rejection of middle-class pre-occupations. What swings into sight, consequently, is the adumbration of a world elsewhere, which Yeats, contrary to Ibsen's pessimism, elevates or prioritizes as preferable even though fatal. As gesture, this action is both romantic and futile; Yeats glorified the visionary failure.

My initial point here is simply to lay down as basis the Ibsenist model in modern Irish drama. Of course, there was the Chekhovian model also, but this came into evidence in Ireland much later (following Edward Martyn's early pioneering productions in Hardwicke Street), in the 1930s and after. But for my purposes here there is no distinction to be made between the two models. In Chekhov, too, we have a hidden dualism, a dialectic whereby an underlying and tragic realm of spiritual truth emerges through a framework of naturalism.

It is perhaps worth recording that Kilroy has adapted both Ibsen and Chekhov to the Irish stage: *Ghosts* (1989) and *The Seagull* (1981). He is not alone in this continuing interest: Frank McGuinness has provided versions of *Rosmersholm* (1987), *Peer Gynt* (1988), *Three Sisters* (1990) and *Uncle Vanya* (1995), while Brian Friel's *Three Sisters* (1982) is but a concrete example of the importance of Chekhov in his work generally. At the same time, Kilroy's adaptations are more concise, because they translate Ibsen literally to Irish conditions.

Of course, it is not to be thought that Kilroy has anything much to do with Ibsen's rather dated dramatic form, the well-made play. It is rather that Ibsen's pioneering concern with the relationship between private individual and public world in all its moral implications continues to have dramatic potential. If that relationship has become a convention, in Raymond Williams's sense of the word,[7] it is an enduring and enabling one. For Kilroy, the central concern is, he says, 'how to relate the integral self of the writer to the society around him'.[8] Since Ibsen, this relationship has been rendered more acute by the destabilizing of the self in the subject-object relationship, leading to what Beckett as early as the 1930s was calling 'rupture of the lines of communiction'.[9] It can be said, however, that Kilroy's concerns, while open to post-modern arguments, stay closer to definably modernist notions of responsibility. In short, he is always closer to the basically moral drama of Ibsen than to the metaphysical mockeries of Beckett.

Thus he goes on to say in that same essay, 'The Irish Writer: Self and Society, 1950-80':

I am fascinated and often appalled by what happens when the intense, concentrated hopes, fears, beliefs of the private person are subjected to the fragmenting, diffusionary effects of public life. I now know that both my works [*Talbot's Box* and *The Big Chapel*] are about that division and that both acknowledge a failure to achieve a wholeness of community in the Irish experience which they describe.[8]

Now I would argue that this clearly stated concern over a community fragmenting under the social, economic and spiritual pressures of contemporary life marks Kilroy's status as part of the Irish tradition. For clarification, take briefly the case of Synge. Avowedly hostile to Ibsen, Synge actually emulated Ibsen's whole naturalistic enterprise. Thus *The Shadow of the Glen* (1903) creates on stage a thoroughly disturbing imitation of rural Irish life, with the simulated death of the husband Dan Burke giving way to a resurrection loaded with irony. That resurrection is nothing but the re-assertion of dominance over Nora, the horror of whose life is more deeply communicated than Ibsen's Nora in *A Doll's House*. Side by side, or underneath, the seeming mundanity of Nora's existence appears a hunger of spirit nowhere to be appeased within the structure of the society she inhabits and the setting defines. Synge's originality, however, lay in his giving to Nora the possibility of a revolutionary conscious-

ness. If that sounds grandiose, and it does, let us accept that
Nora leaves the cottage for the open roads and all they symbol-
ize in Synge. She is expelled, but she goes willingly for in her
going she can cast a judgement on husband and lifestyle. And
she goes in the company of the Tramp. Synge altered his source
to make the Tramp Nora's protector. Together they leave the
settled world for the uncertainties/contingencies and yet the freedom of a world elsewhere. All of this is couched not only in
Synge's marvellous language but in gesture, stance and movement. The two rejected ones, objects, become subjects in their
own right and assume responsibility for their exit from a failed
community. Many of Synge's plays present a similar ending.
Both *The Well of the Saints* (1905) and *The Playboy of the Western
World* (1907) propose an exile from a society exposed as disa-
bling and coercive. What the protagonists exit to is freedom,
though death is also part of the deal. They will become tramps
and outcasts, but also critics of a spiritually bankrupt society.

Kilroy does not, of course, imitate Synge's dramatic idea. The
complex position of the contemporary writer is that he or she
has to relate not only to the world as it is but also to the tradition
which went before. Sean O'Faolain addressed this question rather
interestingly in an editorial in *The Bell* in 1941:

This struggle between the inescapable Past and the insistent Present,
between luxuriating into nostalgia and working out of ambition, has
made itself felt strongly since 1916. If there is any distinct cleavage
among us to-day it is between those who feel that tradition can explain
everything, and those who think it can explain nothing . . . We are living . . . to a great extent experimentally, and must go on doing so.[10]

But here, before launching into an account of Kilroy's first
play in this regard, *The Death and Resurrection of Mr. Roche* (1968),
I have to interject a second major strand in the texture of his
work in general. This is modern British and American drama.
When in 1956 the Royal Court Theatre in London initiated a new
drama with the work of Osborne, Arden, Wesker and others
Irish theatre and Irish writers could not but be affected. It is
commonplace to speak of Osborne's *Look Back in Anger* (1956) as
marking the beginning of a new revolution in modern drama, a
revival of modernism, through the provision of a new voice,
that of the young, disaffected, sardonic but highly articulate
Jimmy Porter. Recently, Osborne's sequel to that epoch-making
if in some respects surprisingly undistinguished drama played

in London: thirty-six years on, Jimmy Porter still lives, in the appropriately titled *Déjà Vu* (1992). The Royal Court, likewise, still lives, and two of Kilroy's plays have played there, one of them actually premiering there, in fact (*The Seagull*). Kilroy visited the Royal Court as a university student and teacher in the 1950s and early 1960s and absorbed not only the sense of excitement, the sense of fresh winds blowing away a generation of cobwebs and inhibitions in the theatre, but also the sense of possibility opened up again by the courageous attitude of George Devine, artistic director.[11] We bear in mind that Devine made the Royal Court available for the premiere of *Fin de Partie* in 1958, shortly to be followed by the English-language premiere of *Endgame*, in which Devine himself played Hamm. This was a bare two years after Osborne's *Look Back in Anger* and Arthur Miller's *The Crucible*, indicating the range of the modernist repertory cultivated by the Royal Court. This cosmopolitan, eclectic, socially aware theatre moulded the sensibility of young Kilroy, already alerted to the affinities between Irish and world theatre through a similar if small-scale Dublin theatre with which he was associated, namely the Pike.[12]

When in 1959 Kilroy called for changes in the Irish theatre, in an article published in *Studies*, he certainly had in mind the example of the Royal Court, for he speaks of 'the idea of community workshop, a club theatre which tries to bring back the writer to the stage without embarrassment to, and in perfect harmony with [,] the players'.[13] This notion of theatre as community, as image of the very healing process which the drama itself indicates is necessary if the alienated state of modern man/woman is to be addressed, is at the core of all of Kilroy's work for the stage. In summary, then, the Royal Court proposed to the young Kilroy a model he could and did follow on two fronts: first of a drama liberated from bourgeois inhibitions and occupied with the plight of modern, post-war man, notably man as outsider, and second, a model of a theatre where the writer is *primus inter pares*, one of a collaborative artistic community, to be sustained by a sense of non-commercial, collective responsibility (George Devine's well-known 'right to fail'). Thus the two dimensions of modernism supporting Kilroy's drama are the Abbey tradition, Ibsenist, rural-based and historically aware, and the more socially focused Royal Court tradition, post-Ibsenist, urban-based, existentially aware, and open to international influences of many kinds (whether American, British or continental).

In Kilroy's first stage play, *The Death and Resurrection of Mr. Roche* (1968), we get the familiar dialectic between hero and world. But all is now ironized. The hero, Kelly, is an uprooted country-man living and working in the metropolis. Tradition, which O'Faolain defined as 'the ritual of life',[14] is something rapidly slipping outside Kelly's grasp. An ageing bachelor, he lives a nightly round of distraction found in drink among companions who care nothing for him. He is getting older but less part of any meaningful community. His world is thus one of empty rituals, a frantic bid to stave off loneliness and awareness of the void. His chief ally is Myles, a trendy car salesman whose phi-losophy is a cheap form of hedonism. His advice is to live only for the pleasure of the moment and to forget about anything savouring of tradition. It is rather like the conflict in Albee's *Who's Afraid of Virginia Woolf?* (1962) where the older man George represents history and the younger man Nick represents biol-ogy.[15] Myles is biological man. He says at one point, 'If there's one thing that gives me the willies it's halloo-hallah about his-tory and stuff. It's now that counts, friend, now and not yesterday'.[16] The naturalism in which the play is framed en-dorses Myles's deadly materialism just as surely as Synge's cottage dramatizes the trap which encloses Nora. In Kilroy's play, too, a death and resurrection motif provides the perspective on an alternative, a world elsewhere. But it is important to note here that Kilroy's attitude towards tradition is a self-aware and a critical one. Where he and his generation of Irish playwrights are aware of the tradition they are equally concerned with inno-vation, and with what Kilroy calls formal inventiveness, so that what emerges should be 'a new kind of theatrical imagination' imposed upon traditional material.[17] Therefore, what is arresting about *The Death and Resurrection of Mr. Roche* is the new and revealing way in which it establishes the dialectic between the actual and the possible.

What this implies is a use of the stage in a style suddenly at variance with the convention used up to this point. When Mr. Roche returns as it were from the dead, the stage direction reads as follows, describing his re-entry to Kelly's flat in the company of his young friend Kevin and the man known as the Medical Student:

They approach like figures in a dance, almost linked, partly to support one another, partly to catch the mood of delirious revelry that grips them. (p. 69)

This return and the narrative of explanation which follows evoke a sense of wonder and even of miracle. To achieve this within the confines of a realistic setting is, as Eliot had found in *The Cocktail Party* (1949) and elsewhere, extremely difficult. Yet it marks the essence of Kilroy's theatre, which is a theatre of transformation. Mr. Roche's presence at the end of the play is a 'Real Presence' in the liturgical sense; he is a figure who sanctifies the space around him. It is ironic that Kelly is still afraid of him and is anxious to be rid of him. This means that Kelly still has not advanced, still is entrapped in his self-made tomb. The play ends with Mr. Roche in sole possession of the space, however, so that the audience is forced to apprehend the space's transformation into a veritable 'Holy Hole', a place where spiritual growth and sanctuary might be allowed.

Kilroy never again confined his drama to the naturalistic convention. What he wanted to say, by way of critique of social values and cultural oppressiveness, requires the resources of a far more experimental notion of staging. In an essay published in 1977, 'Two Playwrights: Yeats and Beckett', he made clear his affinity for a style of theatre which self-consciously accepted its artificiality, which he had by then begun to exploit. For example, he praised in that essay Yeats's use of 'a theatrical ceremony that draws attention to its own stage artifice'.[18] In the Irish tradition, where naturalism has dominated over experimentalism, very few playwrights besides Yeats worked in the alternative modes of symbolism, expressionism and surrealism. Denis Johnston was one of these exceptions, a modernist writer Kilroy admires and has written about.[19] It is fair to say that Johnston's *The Old Lady Says 'No!'* (1929) offered to Kilroy a radical alternative to Synge and the Ibsenist model of theatre. Time and space are disrupted, history is superimposed ironically on the present by means of a play-within-the-play which breaks down and dispels the realistic conventions, and the values of Robert Emmet are re-examined for their mixture of violence and romanticism. Johnston's theatre is a theatre of historical revisionism and his methods, avant-garde in 1929, showed how heroic themes and personalities could be ironically seen again. In *Talbot's Box* (1977) Kilroy for his part presents a revisionist treatment of a saintly man, Matt Talbot, whose private life and obsession with God ran parallel to but ignored all the significant historical events in Ireland before and after the 1916 rising. Kilroy sets the play in modern Ireland, as Johnston had set his, and imagines the relation between Talbot's fanatic individualism and the modern greed to appropriate celebrity and exploit saintliness for ideological ends. In order to dramatize this point Kilroy defied all kinds of realistic conventions. Matt Talbot is first presented as dead, on a trolley in a Dublin morgue; then he comes to life to enact his own history and social entrapment. A priest is played by a woman, while two men, simply named First Man and Second Man, change costumes frequently on stage and enact a variety of roles. A Brechtian style thus casts the story of Talbot's pilgrimage in an ironic light.

Brecht's work came to London in 1956, with the first visit of the Berliner Ensemble, which served to influence such Royal Court writers as John Arden and Edward Bond (and even Osborne's *Luther*, 1961). Even greater notoriety spread from the Brechtian style encrusted by Joan Littlewood's Theatre Workshop onto Behan's *The Hostage* (1958). In *Talbot's Box*, however, the influence of Artaud is probably stronger than that of Brecht. In his essay on Yeats and Beckett Kilroy writes of Artaud with considerable approval, especially of Artaud's notion in *The Theater and its Double* of the stage as 'a concrete physical place which asks to be filled, and to be given its own concrete language to speak'.[20] This concrete language is non-verbal and palpable; it operates on the senses. In *Talbot's Box* the stage design is a huge, slatted box which opens up at the start of the play and closes when Talbot dies in a blaze of suffusing, discomforting light.[21] This image of containment, even of packaging, encapsulates the whole play metaphorically. The audience is kept at a distance and rendered uncomfortable: at times encouraged to laugh, at times to sympathize with Talbot, for all that he is clearly fanatical. Instead, therefore, of a saint play like Eliot's *Murder in the Cathedral* (1936) or Bolt's *A Man for all Seasons* (1960), modernist and humanistic, we get a complex and ambiguous study of theatre itself as accomplice to voyeurism and exploitation. In short, a superb experimental play.

Both heroes, Talbot and Kelly, exemplify Kilroy's basic thesis that the individual in modern Ireland cannot escape the results of a disintegrating community. Synge's option, the defiant gesture of the outcast figure taking to the roads, is no longer feasible (except in the lost landscapes of a Beckett play). The Kilroy hero must register the disintegration, internalize it, and, if he can, create or discover some kind of individual accommodation with it; more likely such discovery is for the audience, who must piece together a possible alternative way, the world elsewhere. Sometimes this dichotomy is presented as a battle between darkness and light. This can take more than one form, private or public. For example, Kelly's vigil takes place through a long night of virtual solitude, until Mr. Roche re-appears with the dawn and offers a new notion of community. Matt Talbot wrestles with the darkness within himself, adding, 'there's no peace till ya walk through it inta some kinda light'.[22] The battle is for wholeness, for identity. But identity is now no simple matter but can even be a fiction, as is stated in *Double Cross*.[23]

In *The Seagull* the broader, cultural implications of self *versus* society are very forcefully expressed. Essentially, the play in Kilroy's translation of Chekhov to the West of Ireland becomes a swan-song of the Ascendancy, incapable of seeing the coming apocalypse. The bewildered would-be writer Constantine, a kind of secularized Matt Talbot, writes a symbolist play to impress his actress mother. In this version it centres on the mythical Battle of Moytura, between the forces of light, the Tuatha de Danaan, and the new forces of darkness, the Firbolgs. In this play-within-the-play Kilroy coherently defines the cultural argument of modernism. Lily (Chekhov's Nina), the actress who speaks the monologue, concludes:

I see him now [Balor] the father of giants as he comes, symbol of base matter and common earth. Where is Lugh, the bright-faced to cast his sling at the terrible eye, to strike it out? . . . When the gods die, man is . . .'[24]

And she never finishes the line, as this is the point when Constantine, because of his mother's interruptions, abruptly cancels the performance. But what she was about to say, surely, was, 'When the gods die, man is destitute', which is the basis of all modern drama, if not all modern literature.

In *The O'Neill*, a play disgracefully left unpublished, Kilroy historicizes this destitution. We are, perhaps, familiar with the story-line because of Brian Friel's later version of the same material in *Making History* (1988). Viewed today, Kilroy's play is altogether prophetic in an uncanny way. Staged in May 1969 it preceded the outbreak in August 1969 of the violence in Belfast which initiated the turmoil from which Ireland has not yet recovered. The play focuses on Hugh O'Neill, the last great leader of the old Gaelic order, who fought, first victoriously and then with disastrous results, to unite the Irish against Elizabeth I and so to restore Ireland's former independence. Unlike Friel, Kilroy shows O'Neill in his greatness, leading up to the Battle of the Yellow Ford in 1598. He is concerned with a man of destiny, but without certainty, a man who describes himself as 'splintered'[25] and as living 'in two worlds, God help me, speak[ing] two languages, serv[ing] two causes'.[26] O'Neill, educated in England and created Earl of Tyrone by the Queen, finds disloyalty a complex issue. He despises the disunity of the native Irish, admires the civilization of the English. He is torn between light and darkness. As he puts it before the climactic (apocalyptic) Battle of Kinsale, Ireland's Actium:

For a long time I didn't know our destiny. I saw a dying race about me, clinging to a dying past. I saw its savagery, its beauty, its nobility, its consuming sickness of the spirit. And then I thought I saw the road out of this darkness. It leads to Kinsale.[27]

The light on the other side is the light of Europe. As O'Neill hopes, 'We can salvage the best of our past among the leaders of a new, united Christian Europe'. But if the Irish lose the battle at Kinsale, O'Neill goes on, 'A darkness will descend upon Ireland'.[28] And so it was to be. The defeat at Kinsale marked the decline of the old Gaelic civilization. What Thomas Kinsella calls 'a broken tradition' was the result.[29] Writing in 1966 Kinsella mourned his own deprivation as poet, his dislocation from a cultural wholeness, beginning, as he puts it, 'in the full light of Gaelic culture and end[ing] in darkness, with the Gaelic aristocracy ruined and the death-blow already delivered to the Irish language'.[30] Brian Friel was waiting around the corner to dramatize this loss once again in *Translations* (1980).

The irony of Kilroy's O'Neill is manifest. He is a casualty of history illustrating what might have been, a world elsewhere. He may owe something to Osborne's Luther, another agonized consciousness poised between the old world and the new. But the main source is, of course, O'Faolain's biography of O'Neill, published 1942, where the European dimension of O'Neill's consciousness is underlined. In the passage already quoted from Kilroy's play, just before the Kinsale débâcle, O'Neill goes on to say that before the Irish could join the new, united Christian Europe they 'have to see themselves transfigured'.[31] They would have in some sense to be re-born, resurrected. There is, perhaps, an element of prophecy in this play in relation of Ireland's joining the Economic Community, which didn't happen until four years later in 1973. After the referendum on Maastricht (1992) that sense of the prophetic is even keener. Irish identity is undergoing a massive transfiguration at present; Kilroy's O'Neill play provides a comment both on its necessity and on its cost.

As are most modern history plays after *Saint Joan* (1923), Kilroy's 'O'Neill' is thus an allegory of specific contemporary conditions. We see a comparable allegory in *Double Cross*, where the thrust is in the opposite direction from 'O'Neill'. Here we have two disloyal Irish leaders of opinion, Brendan Bracken and William Joyce, mirror images of each other as self-made men craving the integrated community each idealizes in the English imperium. 'It's odd, isn't it,' Bracken asks, thereby giving the theme of the play, 'that patriotism and treason may be fuelled by the same hunger for space'.[32] This space is once again the world elsewhere. *Double Cross* was written for and staged by the Field Day Company; its allegorical force appropriately activates a desire for an Ireland commanding pluralist allegiance. In its theatricality, with a single actor playing both Bracken and Joyce, it manipulates perceptions to see identity as something constructed and creative rather than fixed and determined. As always with a Kilroy play, a margin of work is left to the audience in concluding the creative act.

The Madame MacAdam Travelling Theatre (1991) is also a history play set in rural Ireland during World War II (just about the time when Caen was being bombed by the allies, I expect). The travelling players, marooned for lack of petrol, are English, and this is significant. The late Barbara Hayley has written extremely well on this play in *Studies on the Contemporary Irish Theatre* (1991) and she has emphasized its self-conscious theatricality. All I wish to do here is to relate the play to what I've said already and thereby provide some kind of conclusion.

The Madame MacAdam Travelling Theatre is what might be termed a prescriptive play. It is a play about healing and history. Where in his earlier work Kilroy had taken the pulse of the nation, diagnosed various neuroses and chronic ailments, he had only sketched in, like the frail outline one makes of icons on a computer screen, possible remedies. It is noteworthy that the single exception prior to *Madame MacAdam* is also a self-reflexive play which sets up a constant dialogue between theatre and life. This was *Tea and Sex and Shakespeare*, an unpublished play first staged at the Abbey in 1976 and revived in a rewritten form in 1988 by Rough Magic, a young, adventurous Dublin company.

It is essentially a play about writer's block, about a playwright in a panic, whose fantasies, fears and obsessions literally people the stage as he gets through one more day uninspired. (The author, however, contrives to make a play of this failure.) Using surrealist techniques, Kilroy manages to make a nightmare into a hilarious comedy. As the hero struggles with his phantoms, who pop out of a wardrobe or simply walk in through walls, we are never sure when the landlady, her attractive daughter, and her other lodger are actually present – as sometimes they are – or figments of Brien's ongoing fantasies. He is interrupted as often as O'Casey's Donal Davoren, and in his way is just as much a pretender, the shadow of a penman, perhaps. But the variations on illusion and delusion are more to the point here. For example, Brien is making love with his wife Elmina when the landlady Mrs. O. enters with a vase and flower.

BRIEN: Mrs. O! can't you see I'm engaged?
MRS. O: I can see you have your britches down. You poor man. Will
           you pull them up around you!
BRIEN: (Hysteric) You see nothing else?
MRS. O: I'm not looking Mr. Brien. Decency forbids.[33]

Here we both *see* Elmina and must accept she's not there. Then Brien tells Mrs. O. she'll be in his play: 'I want to dispense with real people. Just one or two imagined caricatures like yourself, Mrs. O'. 'That's nice,' she says (p. 51). However, she can't get into the play unless she's changed, 'Transformed, translated. transmuted' (p. 59). The play thus begins to suggest the special powers of art. But it is with Brien's serious neuroses, especially his sexual insecurity and anxiety over Elmina, that the play is mainly concerned. Brien's impotence is a two-way street. 'When I'm writing I can't fuck' (p. 6). But he isn't writing, and hence the quality of French farce unleashed involving unreal persons. If the artist can't produce, so what? Has his pain any reference to society, to the scheme of things? What Kilroy has to say relates to and to an extent replies to Brian Friel's portrait of the artist in *Faith Healer* (1979). Where Friel sees the artist as a random blood donor who might easily do harm to the world's body through his dodgy chromosomes, Kilroy is more optimistic. He draws on Shakespeare to make this process work. If *Othello* is the play which gives vent to Brien's deepest-seated anxiety (jealousy), the later romances, especially *The Tempest*, offer him a way out. Surreal though the action is, it moves to the point where marriage, love, acceptance and forgiveness receive full expression on the stage, as the fantasy characters re-enact Shakespeare's endings one after the other. As the possibilities extend beyond violence, jealousy and evil, the option for love and miracle becomes more credible. Left alone on stage after his fantastic trial Brien starts to type at last. His wife enters, back from her day's work; stage direction:

Brien, tense again, sits up, waiting. Elmina has entered into the light, relaxed, affectionate, coming back from work . . . She kisses him on the top of the head, ruffling his hair and behaves with great warmth towards him. She drapes herself across his work area, with a sigh. (p. 170)

His anxieties clearly have no basis. His wife inhabits his writer's space at her ease; she has the walk of a Muse. Suddenly their being together cancels all that went before, leaving a transformed icon. In contrast, say, to the coy ending of *Look Back in Anger* where Jimmy and Alison retreat into playing bears and squirrels to keep the world at bay we have in *Tea and Sex and Shakespeare* a comic victory over chaos. The audience is brought to experience the very process of creation, its victory over the void. The final note is of ironic collusion, as the audience shares Brien's secret. When Elmina asks, 'Well? How was *your* day?' Brien looks at the audience, 'raises an eyebrow and the play ends' (p. 170). All that matters is that the audience understands what Patrick Kavanagh called 'the secret sign'.[34] The experience of the play is the fellowship of such understanding.

Madame MacAdam tries to extend this diagram of audience-artist-world relationships. Using the device of travelling players (subsequently used by Shane Connaughton in the film *Playboys*, 1992), this play provides two levels of experience which increasingly encroach on each other: the daily lives of a community undergoing the unjustified panic of a possible German invasion and the world of make-believe provided by the actors. From the distance of fifty years all the alarm seems to us ludicrous, from *ludus*, play; so the whole thing is 'comic'. The play doesn't say anything so commonplace as life is theatre or all the world's a stage, but it does *show*, by means of a series of boxes-within-boxes, how necessary a part of experience deceit is. Deceit is play; play is deceit. But play also demands assent, acceptance, tolerance from an audience. The fellowship of the theatrical experience is thus an image of a world elsewhere, a possible community based on understanding and love. The world elsewhere is now the theatre itself. Ironically, this play met with much hostility from the Dublin critics, who thereby refused to see, to accept, what was in front of them.[35] For here Kilroy is combining a history play with a romance to create a world that never was but might be: a pastoral world redeemed or at least redeemable in the imagination, a world not of realism but of deliberate make-believe, where police sergeants understand the business of playing and parish priests are conspicuously absent: a land, indeed, of heart's desire where tradition, rituals, history, pain can all be miraculously transformed. Such is the essentially poetic theatre of Thomas Kilroy, a unique blending of tradition and a very individual talent.

It is clear that the attempt in *The Madame MacAdam Travelling Theatre* is to use theatre in a new yet age-old way. Just as Seamus Heaney fused *Philoctetes* and *The Tempest* to provide an ending for *The Cure at Troy* (1990) which could express a dream of social regeneration,[36] so Kilroy's play, which succeeded Heaney's in the Field Day programme, fused melodrama and Shakespeare to suggest a transcendence of history. Kilroy is an inter-textual writer; he uses theatrical collage with great dexterity. But in the end he is a modernist in a post-modernist world. He wants to use his art to supply images of restoration and completion. With remarkable devotion to the therapeutic obligations of art he has worked consistently to bring into balance the rival claims of the individual psyche and social imperatives, history and contemporaneity, tradition and the individual talent. He stands as an example of the late twentieth-century Irish writer seeking an adequate language to imagine a habitable world elsewhere.

THE CREATIVE PROCESS

Tom Murphy

This paper is about discovering a play in the process of writing it. Discovering the *real* subject as against what turns out to be only the ostensible subject. Discovering something about the self in the creative process; perhaps why I chose to write a particular play in the first place or why the subject chose me.

In writing a play I attempt to create or recreate the *feeling* of life; *ideas* follow and are developed as appropriate: this is a bonus. Why I should want first and foremost to create or recreate the feeling of life is a good question. I am tired of being victim to feeling and would through my characters wrest autonomy for myself, create a new power? I don't know. Perhaps I simply resent waking in the morning to the whim of existence that has already decided I am in good mood / I am in bad mood / I am in-between and, though I cannot do a blessed thing about whatever the allotted state, I can retaliate, declare to whimsical existence, 'Look, I can do it too!'

There are three broad approaches from which one can look at *Famine* and its genesis. It is historical and, I believe, accurate to the historical facts that it presents to the degree of my ability and my judgement in writing a play of this kind. It is autobiographical, the subject offering me the opportunity to write about myself, my private world and my times. It has, as a play, a life of its own and, tired of history, tired of me, it continues its own process of discovery to its own conclusions, now with me, the author, not in the ascendancy, but in pursuit.

The Famine in Ireland in the 1840s was and is the greatest punctuation mark in Irish history. It stopped the Irish race in its tracks. Nature, politics and the victims themselves joined in a conspiracy to ensure its magnitude. Exact records were not kept, were not possible, but it is estimated that there was a loss of two and a half million people.

I first read the facts of the Irish Famine in Cecil Woodham Smith's book, *The Great Hunger*. I was living in London at the time and I believe that that geographical distancing from my roots both objectified and personalised what might otherwise have been a purely emotional, racial response.

The Great Hunger was a major event in the publishing world [1962] and I expected it to inspire a half-dozen plays on the subject of the Irish Famine. I'm still surprised that they did not materialise. In the next couple of years, for my part, the only thing that happened was a call from an out-of-work actor friend who was prolific in ideas for projects for Broadway and whose present one was that he had found a brilliant young musician who would, if I did the libretto, write the music for a big musical to be called 'The Great Hunger'.

But I had a lingering sense of awe about it all, one that was beyond my comprehension – more of an apprehension of the bewilderment and desolation that belongs to a dream.

Another couple of years on, I started to research the Irish Famine. Histories, memoirs, accounts. In fiction I read William Carleton. Carleton, 'the first Irish peasant writer' had set one of his novels, *The Black Prophet*, in earlier famine times and, as well as being a great read, his *Traits & Stories of the Irish Peasantry* is a mine of social history. I knew there was a play there, but where? And the scale of the thing, another time, a nightmare world.

Research tends to perpetuate itself and postpone the writing and, to achieve balance I told myself, I went further afield, to Europe. By no means was Ireland the only place stricken by famine in the mid-19th century. Among other things, I found a book translated from the French, a moving account of famine among the Eskimos in the 1840s; its title, too, was *The Great Hunger*. (The Irish, in the Gaelic, referred to the Famine as *an t-ocras mor*, the big or great hunger; the Eskimos used the same phrase in their language.)

I bought newspapers and magazines for the contemporary scenes of starvation. I read about a famine that was said to be, for three years, raging in Bihar. One Sunday, in *The Sunday Times*, I think, a cross Mrs Ghandi was declaring that, contrary to what was believed and much as it might disappoint people, there was no famine in Bihar. Her story was, perhaps, the correct one. But now, as was pointed out, the astonishing thing was not the existence or non-existence of famine in Bihar but that there should be any doubt in the matter. Another interesting one, again involving India, was when the USA offered to ship its vast surplus of grain to India: then it was discovered that no system of transport could be devised to distribute it. (And how India or Pakistan could mobilise overnight if one declared war on the other! How things are done today in the Gulf!)

And the mediaeval 'Anti Christ' re-emerged in Northern Ireland.

This research, and more, has found resonances in *Famine*.

Perhaps simultaneous with the research but more than likely when the actual writing started, consciously or unconsciously, the thought was emerging that the absence of food, the cause of famine, is only one aspect of famine. What about the other 'poverties' that attend famine? A hungry and demoralised people become silent. People emigrate in great numbers and leave spaces that cannot be filled. Intelligence becomes cunning. There is a poverty of thought and expression. Womanhood becomes harsh. Love, tenderness, loyalty, generosity go out the door in the struggle for survival. Men fester in vicarious dreams of destruction. The natural exuberance and extravagance of youth is repressed . . . The dream of food can become a reality – as it did in the Irish experience – and people's bodies are nourished back to health. What can similarly restore mentalities that have become distorted, spirits that have become mean and broken? Or what price survival?

Even assuming it to be true, it would be foolish to suggest that the moodiness of the Irish personality that is commented on – we blow hot, we blow cold, swing from light to black, black to jet black – stems solely from the Famine, as it would be foolish to suggest that the Irish race was a singularly warm, wild and happy one in pre-famine times. But Famine is a racial memory, it provides a debilitating history and that it has left its mark I have no doubt. And, consciously or unconsciously, rightly or wrongly, another thought/feeling was emerging: Was I, in what I shall call my times, the mid-20th century, a student or a victim of the Famine? It was that thought/feeling, I believe, that made me want to write the play, the need to write about the moody self and my times.

Though I can boast grand moments of under-privilege in my childhood and upbringing I was fed and, so, I cannot boast that I was altogether blighted. I was respectable. The people in my times were not mean, they were respectable. We were unnaturally docile and obedient. Only the bank manager and the three-card-trick man wore a moustache or suede shoes. The powers that ruled over us – the institutions, offices and officers – didn't want trouble and neither did we. We called them, then as now, 'The Authorities'. We were a suspicious and secretive people, shameful of the universal conditions that apply to humankind. Everyone had a sense of inferiority. We were smug about Catholicism, the one true Church. There were occasions when undefined, ingrowing resentment festered into rage and erupted in violence but it was mindless stuff ultimately, more self-destructive than destructive. Breaking from the norm too, occasions when words and the mouths that said them became distorted, sounded and looked ugly, as if at war with their messages, counsel to meekness, obedience, self-control. And though the Blessed Virgin had the right ear of God, still, the greatest moral law of all was sometimes broken when a boy and girl stayed out all night together – in the Race Course in my hometown. The Church authorities did their damnedest about that kind of thing but, in that kind of thing, contrary to exaggerated reports, their job was not so all-consuming or demanding: staying out all night in a race course is exceptional behaviour, as can be imagined. Undoubtedly, the Irish Catholic Church was and is very hot on sex but I do not leave the Irish, sexual preoccupational malady entirely on its doorstep; or the enigma of the great many bachelors about in my times who appeared to be sexless rather than being sexually repressed by any Church or institution.

Eamon de Valera, an Taoiseach (Prime Minister), in a famous, much-commented-on speech, saw us as a happy people, enjoying frugal comforts, with comely maidens dancing at the crossroads. Actually, the comforts were often better than frugal and the comely maidens, though dancers, wouldn't be seen – as some of their great-grandmothers had been seen? – dead at the crossroads. We danced in ballrooms and, depending on the answer to 'What do you do?' we fell in love.

We didn't complain. Nobody wanted 'to go getting their names up'. 'Be wise' could be said to be the slogan of the times. A boy aged twelve – maybe a little more – stole a shilling from the chemist shop where he worked as a messenger boy. He was interrogated by 'The Authorities' and further interrogations were forthcoming. He stole a tin of rat poison out of the same chemist shop, ate it, and died. Only one person in a town of

5,000 people, a woman, complained to 'The Authorities' about it. The system appeared to be working.

The system worked. Emigration was happening on a grand scale. Most families were touched by it; some were decimated, as was mine.

Consciousness of disease was intense. TB (Tuberculosis) was the dreaded one. In retrospect it is amusing. I was into manhood when I discovered one day that momentary alarm had overtaken me at what I was reading. Germs can issue from a mouth at 20,000 miles per second – or some such incredible speed, said *The Readers' Digest*. It was chance, mere luck that had saved me from such determined velocity, not the cunning strategems I had employed. Oh, the need to write about the self, and to conceal the privacies!

There was consciousness of education too and it could be had free if the money wasn't there to pay for it. The teachers, mainly clerics, celibates, so understanding in their willingness to waive fees but so starved of affection in their own lives behaved, with few exceptions, in a brutal manner to the children in their care.

There was another mythology – not de Valera's. Well, maybe it was – about the Travelling People ('Tinkers') who lived in makeshift tents on the roadside. They never used bad language, they were strictly monogamous, and so on. School friends from outlying areas used to talk about passing these tents. I heard a school friend one morning say that he had seen an infant's legs covered with hoar and frost sticking out from under a monogamous tent. Later in life, a man of the Travelling People told me that they had a phrase, 'Fuck or freeze'.

As children, when our street-games went wrong, better than four-letter words of insult to one another was 'Pauper', or 'Tinker'.

Pause for a moment for relief. I should have said at the start that of course there were good times. My eldest brother once told me that I've got it wrong, that I exaggerate. I asked him did he ever dance with a comely maiden at a crossroads. He said he did, often. He was seventeen years older than me; he emigrated in 1939; his first visit home was twenty years later; his equivalent to my times would have been the 1930s. I don't know about the 1930s, so, maybe he did. I hope he did, often.

But I'm talking about famine. My father was a very resourceful man, fond of hunting, shooting and fishing, and he kept a great vegetable garden. He was a carpenter by trade. A dominant memory of him prior to his emigrating is of a man making coffins in his workshop. Sometimes he had to make one on a Sunday – an emergency, I suppose, or a work of mercy; sometimes the coffins were for children. I understand, but I'm surprised, that he did not emigrate earlier. I used to play with the shavings and I loved the smell of pine.

Almost up to manhood I used to visit an uncle who lived alone on his farm in the country. Though he had cutlery and a dresser filled with shining delph, he used his thumbnail to peel a potato – one hand, expert as a sculptor. I was ashamed of that. I used to accompany him to the post-office-cum-pub to collect his pension and meet his pensioner friends. They too had thumbnails and – or so it appeared to me – were bachelors. It was a great supplementary education but I was mostly bored to death, no matter what the perks. They enjoyed these soirées, joking about diverse subjects, from cutting turf to India to handball to their confusion as to whether they were dreaming or not when people they knew gathered round the bed at night, which was 'comical'. Some of them, like my uncles, taciturn, monosyllabic grunts; others, babbling and piping, perhaps in incipient senility.

A few years after my mother was widowed and was living alone I asked her to come and live with me and my family in London, or, to take her pick, live with one or another of her children. Her reply was quiet, she could have been reflecting aloud to herself, and was made strange perhaps by the fact that the conversation was happening in the small hours of the morning: 'I was born here, I'll die here and I'll rot here'. It gave me a shiver; simultaneously, it excited me and I felt an immense pride in her.

John Connor and Mother in *Famine* are not my mother and father, that is not the point. Consciously and unconsciously, in the writing of the play, while aware of the public event that was the Irish Famine in the 1840s, I was drawing on the private well and recreating and reimagining moods and events, apprehensions of myself and my own times.

And, incidentally, in terms of the dialogue, my problems were no more, no less than in writing plays set in modern times.

The main characters are as rounded as I could make them. They are each given further individuality by having a dominant line to follow in their attempts to survive. Mother tries to live by facing the reality of what is happening; Mickeleen, literally, by spite (until, unfortunately for himself, he becomes interested in

John Connors' so-called 'moral right'); Liam, the most reason-
able of them all, by his natural intelligence; Dan, by conversation
– he is alive as long as he can hear himself talking; and so on. It
was difficult in the usual way of writing to bring this along, but
nothing so difficult as John Connor.

The main thrust of the emerging story was beginning to hang
on John Connor and I didn't know that I wanted that; as a life-
line he was choosing a form of pacifism: I didn't know that I
wanted that either. Considering the scale of the calamity, I suppose I did not think him grand enough for special attention; and
I suppose, too, that my personal sense of outrage was not what I
thought it to be – controlled – and he was not sufficient to it. I
resisted him; the play went on insisting; I looked elsewhere for
an alternative, to characters who did not make the end of a draft
and, for instance, to the violent (and psychopathic?) Malachy. (In
one draft I promised Maeve to Malachy – as a sort of reward, I
suppose, for his violent retaliatory course of action.) The play –
and Malachy – refused.

My problem with John Connor, I now consider, was that he
appeared to be too *ordinary*. He is not stupid, but Liam, Mother
and Mickeleen are all more intelligent. He is a reluctant leader;
leadership embarrasses him, impels him into outbursts of unrea-
sonable resentment and into retreats of moody introspection. He
is a physical force man, one of the 'mad and vicious Connors'
who would, if it came to a confrontation (it nearly does at one
point) be more than a match for Malachy. He is expected to come
up with a 'brave' plan, instead of which he espouses a pacifist
line. (Yes, good drama: he is now 'at war' with the crisis and
also with his own nature.) But he is *not* a moral man. Or moral
in the sense that we know it. He espouses a pacifist line *for
himself*. Increasingly he is now declaring he must do only 'what's
right', inures himself in this abstract which, at best, he only half-
comprehends, gobbledygooks and blusters about it to compel
himself to swallow it. All the while, Mother, his wife, can only
look reality in the face, use her practical resources, which include stealing, to protect him and her family.

He appears to be blind to that, even refusing to acknowledge
the ruin that literally gathers around him. Instead, he begins to
affect a drunken regality and presents himself as a man invested
in some greater truth.

I didn't understand him. And plays I had seen and read –
epic plays – appeared to be unrelentingly consistent and grand

in movement and main character. John Connor in my play, by comparison, appeared to be contradictory, selfish, dishonest, questionable rather than questioning – ordinary. Still, I didn't like those other plays I had seen and read!

It is easy for a writer to become a snob, feel superior to his material. Had I thought of going back to my own times – or to anybody's times – I *might* have found a solution. I might, for instance, have thought of demonstrators protesting, marching for their rights without *necessarily* knowing *what rights*; yes, having a day out as well, but *marching*; people marching in Corpus Christi processions without necessarily believing in Christ, his body or his bride, the Church: but, nevertheless, *marching* – for something. Or I might have remembered gathering with others as spectators to see the 'Tinkers' seemingly mindlessly and, yes, drunkenly, beating up one another; or to see one of them brutally beating up his wife, then strutting, marching about, arms and legs splaying in displaced exhibition, eyes bulging in defiance. Defiance of what? Our morality, is it? Outraged, bewildered humanity, looking for something better than itself?

The contradictions and the complexities – the extremes – in people who are ordinary and who are abject.

I didn't go back to anybody's times for the resolution to my problem with John Connor (and consequently with the whole play), rightly so. A play is a play and it must have its say. The creative process consists mostly of sustained, intensive, plodding work that runs itself to earth every now and again, then follows the full stop, the writer can't go on. Perhaps, perhaps, perhaps, this is interpreted as an act of humility on the part of the conscious mind, and, in acknowledgement or as a reward, a higher authority enters. The Play or, call it, Inspiration. A moment of inspiration, magical to the writer, can be meaningless to everyone else. In the case under consideration a moment happened one day in the form of two words combining, 'sacred' and 'strength'. No one as far as I know who has read or seen, acted in or directed *Famine* has commented on 'sacred strength' and there is no reason why anyone should. It is a matter between the writer and the Play; and the thrill, or at least part of it, is in the surprise of the obvious. It is not necessarily infallible, but 'sacred strength' made thrilling sense to me, artistic and otherwise. John Connor stumbles on to his sacred strength: he dresses it in cant because he does not understand it: it is an instinct to survival, above morality as we know it, a resource greater than his own mere existence or his family's existence, so elemental that it is sacred.

These rare moments do not resolve everything, of course, but when they happen the writer continues the plodding pursuit with greater respect for the characters and the play.

As well as refusing Malachy romance with Maeve, the Play deliberately refused to conclude Malachy's story. It took me some time to come to terms with this too. 'Some say Malachy is dead too: I don't know. Some say he's in America, a gang to him', is the last reference to Malachy in the Play. The line is loaded, albeit in subtext. Malachy is alive but the action of the Play cannot accommodate all of his story because he is the violent consequences of famine. (As the play's different levels began to find the overall balance, I saw Malachy as a foretaste of the atrocities that were to follow in the Land Wars; I saw him, also, as a precursor in a direct line that led to Michael Collins, the great, decisive, guerrilla leader who came seventy-or-so years later.) And, of course, Malachy is the personification of a revenge-theme taken up by other characters. Or, he has gone to America where, like other Irish emigrants, he becomes a gangster and fathers gangsters, like Machinegun Kelly or Legs Diamond – Capone-like. Whichever, he is a violent part of the future.

I don't particularly like 'messages' and I did not set out to say that the resultant of a shameful present is a violent future; it can hardly be said to be novel. I agree with it, of course; the play keeps coming up with it. (Even – though undesignedly – anticipating the outbreak of hostilities in Northern Ireland.) The Parish Priest, a sophisticated and educated man, finds it difficult to sustain his belief in idealism, in view of the inhumanity he sees about him. Maeve's tears at the very end of the play represent hope; her line prior to this, however, is, 'There's nothing of goodness or kindness in this world for anyone but we'll be equal to it yet.' She is a sixteen-year old girl. And, though senile, the affable Dan turns the loving Redeemer on his head: 'As Jesus was noble and denied he has long since been repaying the closed doors to him in Bethlehem!'

Finally on *Famine*. I don't think that a play can do 'justice' to the actuality of famine: in attempting to acknowledge that and in writing-instinct, the time-frame of the play concludes the action in Spring, 1847: the historical worst was yet to come, Black '47.

MEN, WOMEN AND THE LIFE
OF THE SPIRIT IN
TOM MURPHY'S PLAYS

Lynda Henderson

It is very clear that, in a variety of manifestations, the chief concern of Tom Murphy's work as a writer is with the life of the
spirit. By this I mean the sense that, beyond the mundane business of being alive – struggling, suffering, damaging, surviving
– there is the possibility of achieving a redemptive generosity
and love in a secular nirvana. The continuing work of the play
is, to quote J.P.W. King in *The Gigli Concert*, 'to possibilise the
possible' through coming to understand, accept and release mor-
tal, human good. This is specifically the purpose of 'The Gigli
Concert' where, as one of the characters, Man, says to J.P.W.
King:

'When I listen to him (Gigli) – I-can't-stop-listening-to-him! Fills me.
The-things, the-things inside. Tense, every thing more intense. And I
listen carefully. And it's beautiful. But it's screaming – And it's longing.
Longing for what? I don't know whether it's keeping me sane or driving me crazy.'

In *The Sanctuary Lamp*, Francisco says:

'Yeh. I think about all the flesh in the world. And all the hopes. And the
prayers, and all the passions of the passions, in heaps higher than all the
cathedrals, burning in a constant flame. And my heart's the fuse keeps
them burning, and if it blows, so does the lot. That's what I think about'.

This release of a human good is often seen as being achiev-
able only by sand-blasting away the spiritual and psychological

encrustations imposed on Irish society by the long dominance of
a demeaning religious doctrine. Malachy, the central character in
On the Inside, tells Kieran:

'Not only are you a romantic – like the poet Yeats – but, in my opinion,
the famed Irish celibate personality has been imparted to you. Hold on!
Look at it this way. From birth to the grave, Baptism to the Extreme
Unction there's always a celibate there somewhere, i.e., that is, a priest,
a coonic. Teaching us in the schools, showing us how to play football,
taking money at the ballroom doors, not to speak of preaching and
officiating at the seven deadly sacraments.'

The theatrical realisation of this demolition often gives voice
to Murphy's characteristic, refreshing, humanising iconoclasm.
Francisco, the most active protagonist in *The Sanctuary Lamp*,
tells Maudie:

'Right. God made the world, right? And fair play to him. What has he
done since? Tell me. Right. I'll tell you. Evaporated himself. When they
painted his toenails and turned him into a church he lost his ambition,
gave up learning, stagnated for a while, then gave up even that, said
fuck it, forget it and became a vague pain in his own and everybody
else's arse.'

Murphy's protagonists therefore advance simultaneously on
several fronts. They are heroes, braving the unknown on a variety of quests. They are builders, digging foundations in this new
experiential territory; and they are members of a demolition gang,
clearing old structures for new sites.

The title of this paper suggests that men and women are not
seen as equal partners in this work but play highly differentiated
roles. Almost in the traditional organisation of construction teams,
it is the men who do the heavy jobs of metaphorical building
and demolishing; and the women who play the supporting roles
of literal catering, managing, conniving. In *A Crucial Week in the
Life of a Grocer's Assistant* it is John Joe who confronts and re-
solves the issue of a constructive relationship to his home place.
Mother cooks, irons, schemes and keeps his bicycle tyres pumped
up – allowing him the space for his hero-journey. In *The Gigli
Concert* it is J.P.W. who faces up to the abyss and wrenches from
it a redemptive love of humanity:

'The soul of the singer is the subconscious self'; 'Do not mind the pigsty,
Benimillo, mankind still has a delicate ear . . . that's it . . . sing on forever'.

It is Mona who keeps him supplied with food, drink, plants and sex, even in the face of her own despair as she confronts a terminal disease. In *Conversations of a Homecoming*, Tom, the schoolteacher descends through the stages of mystical purification and experiences nihilism and contempt for humanity as it is to be found in his closest companions. Peggy, his fast ageing forty year old 'girlfriend' plays the straight-man to his rages, attempts to heal the wounds he inflicts on his friends by making banal conversation and patiently accepts the brutality of his insults to her. In *Famine* it is John Connor who, John Proctor like, attempts – in the face of the most unthinkable and increasing physical deprivation and death – to live by his own standards of moral probity and social responsibility. It is Mother, his wife, who becomes monstrous through her mean and petty scrimping and saving, grudging everyone everything, stealing – even at death's door – to feed and protect the family as best she can.

In a theatrical as well as a thematic sense, it is usually the female characters who support the central male ones. In *On the Outside*, the character Anne simply provides the reason for Frank's desperation to get into the dance hall when he hasn't the price of a ticket. It is this unfulfilled desperation which drives from his bitter denunciation of the social scheme of things:

'You know, it's like a big tank. The whole town is like a tank. At home is like a tank. A huge tank with walls running up, straight up. And we're at the bottom, splashing around all week in their Friday night vomit, clawing at the sides all around. And the bosses – and the big-shots – are up around the top, looking in, looking down. You know the look? Spitting. On top of us. And for fear we might climb out someway – Do you know what they're doing? – They smear grease around the walls.'

There are always women inhabitants of the various worlds of Murphy's plays – even in his most aggressively masculine play, *A Whistle in the Dark* there is one woman – Betty, the English wife of Michael the son who has left Ireland to make a new life in Coventry. Men are not quite so ubiquitous. In *Bailegangaire*, there is a world only of women – the semi-senile Mommo and her two granddaughters, Mary and Dolly. This omnipresence of women in the plays suggests that the writer is sharply aware of their central role in life – and perhaps too, in art. The director Pam Brighton has remarked that women on stage are always interesting. In theatre, as in life, they can be useful.

However, the female characters rarely have anything of any

real substance to say, (in fact, they have relatively little to say in terms of simple volume). They certainly have almost nothing to offer to the metaphysical debate which provides the raison d'être for the central male characters and for the work as a whole. They are excluded from the abstract, spiritual dimension. Since the hero-journey involves the penetration of the world of the unknown, Murphy has not chosen to exercise positive discrimination in the creation of female heroes. Perhaps the closest he comes to granting a woman entry to the metaphysical is with the young orphan girl, Maudie, in *The Sanctuary Lamp*. When she is telling Harry, with whom she is sharing refuge in the church, that, at home, she scales the lamp posts in the street to attract attention from other children she says:

'Sometimes I'd climb even higher than the light. I would catch the iron thing on top and pull myself up over the top, and sit there in the night. And sometimes, if I waited up there long enough, everything made – sense.'

The association with St Simeon Stylites is almost explicit. Maudie, here, is a woman who has sometimes sought and found enlightenment. Immediately after this, it seems as if Murphy is about to take the character even further – into a spiritually enlarging and humanist fusion of the sacred and the profane:

'Sometimes I'd come sliding down and then I'd do cartwheels . . . or stand on my head. . . . Or there were another. I'd come sliding down, I wouldn't have stopped but keep on running into our house, and I'd open the window, and I'd have stood on the table, and I'd've took off my clothes, and stuck my bottom out at them. and they'd be cheering Maudie, Maudie, Maudie and the two bigger boys . . . Yes, Maud, Maud, come out a minute. Sort of whispering.'

The exultation of the spirit expressed in the cartwheels, in the oneness of mind and body, seems to lead into an essentially innocent advertisement of sexuality. But no. Maudie too has had 'the famous Irish celibate personality imparted' to her, is crushed by the guilt and sense of sin that has been bred from a pregnancy and the death of the child. At the end of the play Maudie literally vanishes – falling asleep in the horizontal Confessional box, while Francisco and Harry redeem their pasts. There is a suggestion that her sleep symbolises her own resolution and release yet, while this may be true to a degree, the theatrical fact is that she is not present to share in or contribute to the general, self-conferred absolution through acceptance.

It might be said – and quickly – that *Bailegangaire* must give the lie to the proposition that Murphy's female characters inhabit a secondary sphere of being and contribute only supporting roles to the dramas. It is, after all, a play where all the characters are women and therefore they must, in volume, account for the entirety of the dialogue – as they do; and must have significant things to say, unless it is suggested that the play is a waste of time – which it is not.

For the purposes of this argument, let us identify three levels of consciousness – of the here-and-now (the superficial and absorbing business of living); of the undergrowth, the reach of the past into the here-and-now, (involving blame, responsibility, guilt, exorcism); and of, in Murphy's words, 'the possible', the unknown, the felt but not seen (the metaphysical, the mystical, the spiritual).

The last of these remains the one closed to Murphy's female characters. The women in *Bailegangaire* are concerned – obsessed even – with the first and the second. For each of them the here-and-now is all but untenable. Mommo is incontinent, bedridden, senile – utterly dependent on granddaughters whose attachment to caring for her is unstable. Mary – the eldest granddaughter who left to become a nurse but who came back home out of some inarticulate awareness of belonging nowhere else – is stuck alone in the remote cottage to look after Mommo. Lonely, loveless, unappreciated, even unrecognised by Mommo, her wretchedness is unthinkable. Dolly, the other granddaughter, is trapped in a meaningless marriage supported only by regular payments from her absent husband. She provides for the texture of her existence by sleeping often and casually with a variety of local men. She is currently pregnant through one of these encounters and dreading her husband's violent reaction when he comes home to discover it. Her concerns are almost exclusively with her own survival in the here-and-now.

For each of them, the reach of the past into the here-and-now is very real and is manifest in Mommo's repeated attempts to tell a particular story. Until she has told it – all of it – she remains, in a way, unshriven in that she cannot forgive herself through acceptance. Mary, whose identity is constantly denied by Mommo's inability – or refusal – to recognise her, also needs the story to be told. She has her own resolution to seek. Mommo's attempts on the narrative form most of the matter of the play and, evidently, the pattern has always been one where she refuses to finish the story and therefore is continually beginning again. This long-running repetition of the main body of the story means that both granddaughters are so familiar with it that they can tell it for her verbatim – and do so, either when she tires or to provoke her to continue when she becomes evasive.

The story is their collective story – up to the point where a series of life-disasters left living only the three of them from their family. Mommo tells the story in the third person – rather as a child does but also perhaps in an attempt to try to see her own role objectively.

In the protracted and interrupted scene which forms the play, Mary, at breaking point, has resolved that this time Mommo will be made to finish the story. She delays giving her the soporific milk drink and persists in waking the old woman from the sleep she has assumed as her escape. Finally, the story is finished and, for the first time, Mommo has had to confront the fact that the third grandchild, Tom the brother of Mary and Dolly, died horribly in a fire caused by himself when the grandparents (Mommo and Seamus) had left them alone while they engaged in a laughing competition in a pub. Mommo's fiction, endlessly propagated in her senile, uncompleted ramblings, has previously been that Tom is living in Galway. When the truth is told, there is an exorcism of long-buried guilt and responsibility; a release from the bonds of the past which, for the first time, allows Mommo to recognise Mary – an admission of her identity which brings a rare moment of grace to a stark scenario. The play ends with the three women together in the one bed, able at last to sleep when the past is spent. Dolly's coming baby represents a future, freed from that past.

The profundity of the matter of the play speaks for itself – even in this abbreviated and selective account. It shows three women, each in thrall to the influence of a suppressed past – needing to find a means of assimilating that past into the here-and-now in order to be reconciled to the present.

However, much as it plumbs the complex realities of life and suffering – some of which are, by gender, out of the male arena – the play does not open to the women the third level of consciousness – of the metaphysical. *Bailegangaire*, therefore does not provide a central exception to the levels of existence inhabited by Murphy's female characters.

If the general role allotted to women in the plays is that of the support group, one would have assumed that this role would be seen as a life-enhancing, warm and welcome one. Not so. It is the role of the toiler, the fixer, the joyless, the charmless, the *necessary*. It is a role openly resented by the men, (sometimes because they are forced to share in the stresses of the women's condition – as when Margaret in *On the Inside*, tells Kieran of her fear that she might be pregnant, causing him to experience her bleak anticipations, before telling him that she has since had a negative diagnosis from her doctor). It is a role the playing of which seems to deform the women; and it is not necessarily a rational role. In *A Crucial Week in the Life of a Grocer's Assistant*, Mother, having bewailed the lack of help offered her by the men in the house, prevents John Joe from getting the bath and the water for her, in case he might get himself dirty. (The demands of the role itself may well provide a defence for the inability of the women to move into the metaphysical plane – there is too much mundane work to be done, too many worries and responsibilities to find the mental freedom to leap beyond.) It is a role grudgingly accepted by men as being indispensable. The character, Man, in *The Gigli Concert*, says to J.P.W. King:

'Supposing my life depended on it, who would I turn to? I went through mothers, brothers, relations. The wife. It all boils down to the wife for us all in the end.'

Somehow, the admission that 'it all boils down' to the wife in the end, seems a spiritually mean and reductive rendering of the essential, and suggests the inevitable in a context where an alternative would have been welcome.

Beyond this begrudging – worse indeed – women are seen as venomous. In *A Crucial Week in the Life of a Grocer's Assistant*, John Joe says to Mother:

'The house is filled with your bitterness and venom. A person can hardly breathe in that street. I don't know what started it. Whether it's just badness or whether it came from a hundred years ago, or whether it's your idea of sex, or whether it's – (Mother is crying) – No, you'll listen to me.'

Women are also seen as conniving and terrifyingly single minded in their loving. In *Too Late For Logic*, the central character Christopher defends his decision to leave his wife by saying:

'I packed a satchel and left to become a scholar to escape the pain of boundless love.'

In *A Crucial Week in the Life of a Grocer's Assistant*, Mother informs on her own cousin, Alec, to the authorities – telling them about the income from his shop which he had not declared in his application for a pension. She thinks that he will then be required to choose one of the two forms of income and that this will pressure him into retiring earlier than he wants from his business in favour of her son, John Joe. She is afraid that, without something to keep him at home, John Joe will go to London. In the end she goes even beyond this manoeuvring. She forces Alec to retire and to give the shop to her son. John Joe is horrified to discover the extent of her blind, relentless love for him.

The sheer strength of the life force in the women is remarkable and daunting. Rather than the noisily insistent John Joe, it is the previously invisible Agnes, in *A Crucial Week*, who quietly sees through her plans to get out of the small town and leave for Boston. In the same play, Mother absorbs the pain of John Joe's assessment of her, yet still plots and schemes to safeguard his material future. In *The Gigli Concert*, with no children, no lover no support and little hope, it is Mona who has the steel to go unaccompanied into hospital to confront the cancer of her lymphatic glands. In *Bailegangaire*, Mommo has survived a series of dreadful human losses and continuing misery, yet still has the energy and the will to keep attempting to assimilate her past. Mary has nothing but the calibre of her character to keep her going through her empty and thankless incarceration with the rambling Mommo. The pregnant Dolly is facing a potentially murderous physical violence from her returning husband yet still raids the hedgerows for the temporary satisfaction of snatched sexual pleasure. In *Famine*, it is Mother – the symbolically named wife of John Connor – who scrapes a bitter survival for her brood until she is defeated; who watches their progressive, wretched deaths. Finally, in an almost fully absurd solution to her predicament, she escapes from the dependence which she sees life as having assigned her, by choosing the moment and manner of her death and that of her last son. She compels Connor to beat them to death, as an act of mercy.

Alongside this strength, women are seen as dishonourable. Many are promiscuous and unfaithful – even the young, like Maudie in *Sanctuary*, who is described by her grandfather as 'a whore's melt' – a brutal reference to her dead mother. In a witty piece of anthropomorphism, the behaviour of the Virgin Mary herself – totemised by convention – is reconsidered in a similar frame. In *Sanctuary*, Harry says of her to Maudie:

'I haven't much time for her either. Mary. It was a good idea alright: holy family, y'know? – the three of them. But see that expression of hers? I know someone like that. And she was a Catholic too. But of course it was all a front to conceal a very highly strung neurotic nymphomaniac.'

Many of the male characters in the plays are far from admirable, yet Murphy takes pains to defend and excuse them where he leaves our reading of their female equivalents to chance and circumstance. In *On the Outside*, Joe is described as: 'immature and irresponsible but not bad'. Frank is presented with the qualification: 'It is hard to say how far he is really bad and how far he is only an intelligent product of his environment'. In *Sanctuary*, Francisco is said to be: 'Irish, self-destructive, usually considered a blackguard, but there are reasons for his behaviour'. This partiality on the part of the writer is extended through the good offices of some of his characters. In *Sanctuary*, just before he libels the Virgin Mary, Harry develops a strong sense of male fellow-feeling for Joseph:

'I've always had a soft spot for Joseph. I've always felt he must have been a bit lonely. Though, mind you, there's some that say she had other children. Quite a large family of them in it, I've heard a person say, so, maybe one of them had a bit of time for him. Joseph. I've always taken an interest.'

This masculine solidarity, evidenced in Murphy's protectiveness of his male miscreants is elevated to a genuinely uplifting, humanist level of metaphysics in Francisco's outburst towards the end of the same play. He declares, from the pulpit in the church during their long night of resolution:

'I have a dream, I have a dream. The day is coming, the second coming, the final judgement, the not too distant future, before that simple light of man: when Jesus, Man, total man, will call to his side the goats – "Come ye blessed! " Yea, call to his side all those rakish, dissolute, suicidal, fornicating goats, taken in adultery and what-have-you. And proclaim to the coonics, blush for shame, you blackguards, be off with you, you wretches, depart from me ye accursed complicated affliction!

And that, my dear brother and sister, is my dream, my hope, my vision and my belief.'

The language in which these soon-to-be-redeemed 'goats' are described seems to carry a subliminal sense of their predominant masculinity – 'rakish, dissolute, suicidal, fornicating'. There is a subtext that the route to redemption for female reprobates will not be so welcomingly smoothed. This subtext sometimes subtly associates them with the fallen – and with the female agent of the fall – through the extent to which they are *knowledgeable*. In *The Gigli Concert*, Man remembers the predatoriness of his first sexual encounter, literally at the hands of the knowing Maisie Kennedy.

What is the problem with women? Why should they be denied entry to, activity in and contribution to the metaphysical dimension? Why should their role in life be accepted so grudgingly as irreplaceable? Why should attitudes to them betray elements of dislike and fear, behind the respect that so reluctantly cannot be denied them?

Among the things that might go toward explaining this are some factors, mundane and mystical. Perhaps there are fears, resentments and jealousies generated by the domestic power that inevitably devolves upon women through the central need for the roles they play in life.

There may be a degree of subliminal fear evidenced in the mythological notion of the vagina dentata to which the Irish phenomenon of Sheela na Gig attests. Certainly, although many of Murphy's male characters talk energetically and enthusiastically about sex, there are plenty of circumstances where they are less than keen to take advantage of fortuitous circumstances. John Joe, in *A Crucial Week*, gives voice to a macho assertion to his Mona that: 'A bird in the hay is worth two in the dance hall', yet his lack of actual activity leads Mona to say plaintively: 'Do you know, you're an awful bad court? I was surprised . . .' At the end of *On the Inside*, Malachy decides to have another drink in preference to a woman and the play closes with his quizzical singing: 'What is this thing called love?' In *The Gigli Concert*, Mona is always having difficulty in energising J.P.W. when she arrives to bed him. Thought is, for him, a more attractive – and less terrifying? – occupation.

Beyond this, perhaps there may be even deeper and more irrational fears that are triggered by the sexual nature and role of women. (Certainly Murphy constantly refers to the lively sexual activity and fertility of many of his female characters). In the ritual process, the Shaman goes on his trance journey to the illud tempus – the primal time of ordering. The participants cannot accompany him on that journey. He alone is equipped to undertake it. Nevertheless, he tries to give them a vicarious experience of it by miming what is happening to him and mimicking his exchanges with the deities he meets there. In the successful completion of the experience, he returns to the world of the spectators, bearing a boon for the common good which he has won in his negotiations with the spirits of the illud tempus.

One of the most illuminating models for the interpretation of theatre is described by David Cole in his book, *The Theatrical Event*. This offers the ritual process as an analogy for the theatrical process. The ritual space translates to the performance space, similarly invested with meaning. The audience are the spectator/participants in the ritual. The play is the agent of transportation by which the audience are removed from their own time and place and taken to another. The actor is the Shaman, often assuming an identity and a shape other than her or his own in order to make the journey to the otherworld of the play. The audience cannot accompany her or him on the journey but the staging of the play allows them to know of its nature, trials and successes. The ending of the play should be the provision of a perceived boon for the community of the audience – an understanding, a catharsis, a new insight perhaps.

In noting the persistence of the anti-theatrical prejudice in society (wonderfully documented by Jonas Barish in his book, *The Anti-theatrical Prejudice*), Cole proposes that we feel uncomfortable in the presence of actors in their everyday identities – in much the same way as members of the tribe kept a working distance from the Shaman in his daily, mundane manifestation – because we know that they have been involved with the mysteries. They know too much. They have been somewhere we cannot go and have been touched by the reverberations of that place.

If we think of the sexual function of women in society in this light, it may offer another explanation for the general ambivalence found in the male attitude to them. Children are born of women in a process and after a journey which they must undertake alone. They return to us with this boon for the common good – a new life. Men can watch their journey and can be given information about it, but cannot share it. The heart of it remains a mystery which no man can experience. As we are all uneasy with Shamen and with actors, men are uncomfortable with women because women know what cannot be known to men. (One of the greatest deforming consequences of Christianity may well be the embedded cultural ambivalence in our evaluation of the possession of knowledge.)

It is a curiosity that, where the life-role of women is shaminic in its child-bearing, Murphy evens the score in the world of his dramas, where only the men have a shamanic role. There can be no doubt that the fullest, most potent and most literal of all such roles is that of J.P.W. King in *The Gigli Concert*. At the end of the play, with the traditional shamanic use of artificial stimulants (vodka and mandrax) to assist in the achieving of the trance state, J.P.W. confronts the limiting deity of the Christian *illud tempus* and, in the catharsis of his humanist defiance, achieves his own enlightenment and resolution:

'The soul of the singer is the subconscious self. Realistic thinking, honest desire for assistance. (*To heaven.*) Rather not. You cut your losses on this little utopia of greed and carnage some time ago, my not so very clever friend. (*To the floor.*) Assist please. In exchange – (*Another square of bread and jam with pill into his mouth and washes it down with vodka.*) And wait, wait, wait . . . and wait . . . until the silence is pregnant with the tone urgent to be born. (*Faintly – and as an echo from a distance – orchestral introduction for the aria "Tu Che A Dio Spiegasti L'Ali". Whispers:*) What! Yesss! Thank you. But just a mo. (*Gestures, cueing out music, takes another pill, a decision against further vodka.*) Stops taking alcohol, purity of potion, contentment in abstinence, care of personal appearance. Diminishing fears of unknown future . . . Resolution fixed in mind for possibilising it. Increase in control to achieve it . . . Abyss sighted! All my worldly goods I leave to nuns. Leeeep! (*Leap*) Pluh-unnge! (*Plunge*) . . . (*Sigh of relief.*) Aah! Rebirth of ideals, return of self-esteem, future known.'

He then 'possibilises the possible' and the voice of Gigli emanates from his throat as he sings the aria to its conclusion. The return of self-esteem has been the agent of redemption, has made it possible for him to find love – for his fellow man – for the first time – an event presaged in Murphy's first solo play, *On the Inside*, where Malachy says:

'Self-contempt is the metaphysical key. How can you, I ask myself, love someone, if, *if*, first, you do not love yourself? How can you do it?'

It would be pertinent, if impertinent, to suggest that, by his own formula, Murphy's apparent difficulty in finding an un-equivocal love for women has its root in an as-yet-incomplete quest first fully to love himself. He has reason to pursue the quest. He is himself a conjuror of magic. As J.P.W. says in *The Gigli Concert*:

'What is magic? . . . simply new mind over old matter.'

Murphy's irrefutably new mind repeatedly transmutes old matter through the alchemy of his writing; and, from his own dangerous and strenuous Shaman-journeys he has brought us back the enduring boon of a humanist resolution.

III.

THE IRISH NOVELISTS
AND THE CREATIVE PROCESS

READING AND WRITING

John McGahern

I came to write through reading. It is such an obvious path that I hesitate to state it, but so much confusion now surrounds the artistic act that the simple and the obvious may be in need of statement. I think reading and writing are as close as they are separate. In my case, I came to read through pure luck.

There were few books in our house, and reading for pleasure was not approved of. It was thought to be dangerous, like pure laughter. In the emerging class in the Ireland of the 1940s, when an insecure sectarian state was being guided by a philistine church, the stolidity of a long empty grave face was thought to be the height of decorum and profundity. 'The devil always finds work for idle hands,' was one of the warning catch phrases.

Time was filled by necessary work, always exaggerated: sleep, Gaelic football, prayer, gossip, religious observance, the giving of advice – ponderously delivered, and received in stupor – civil war politics, and the eternal business that Proust describes as 'Moral Idleness'. This was confined mostly to the new emerging classes – civil servants, policemen, doctors, teachers, tillage inspectors. The ordinary farming people went about their sensible pagan lives as they had done for centuries, seeing all this as one of the many veneers they had to pretend to wear, like all the others they had worn since the time of the Druids.

During this time I was given the free run of the Moroney's library. They were Protestants. Old Willie Moroney lived with his son, Andy, in their two-storied stone house, which was surrounded by a huge orchard and handsome stone outhouses. Willie must have been well into his eighties then, and Andy was about forty. Their natures were so stress-free that it is no wonder they were both to live into their nineties. Old Willie, the beekeeper, with his great beard and fondness for St Ambrose and Plato, 'the

Athenian bee, the good and the wise ... because his words glowed with the sweetness of honey', is wonderfully brought to life in David Thomson's *Woodbrook*.

Willie had not gone upstairs since his wife's death, nor had he washed, and he lived in royal untidiness in what had once been the dining room, directly across the stone hallway from the library, that dear hallway with its barometer and antlered coat rack, and the huge silent clock. The front door, with its small brass plate shaped into the stone for the doorbell, was never opened. All access to the house was by the back door, up steps from the farmyard, and through the littered kitchen to the hallway and stairs and front rooms.

David Thompson describes the Moroneys as landless, which is untrue, for they owned a hundred and seventy acres of the sweetest land on the lower plains of Boyle, itself some of the best limestone land in all of Ireland. The farm was beautifully enclosed by roads which ran from the high demesne wall of Rockingham to the broken walls of Oakport. The Moroneys should have been wealthy. They had to have money to build that stone house in the first place, to build and slate the stone houses that enclosed the farmyard, to acquire the hundreds of books that lined the walls of the library: David Thompson, though, is right in spirit, for Willie and Andy had all the appearance of being landless.

Most of Andy's time was taken up with the study of astronomy. Willie lived for his bees. He kept the hives at the foot of the great orchard. They both gathered apples, stored them on wooden shelves in the first of the stone houses of the farmyard, and they sold them by the bucketful, and seemed glad enough for the halfcrowns they received. As a boy, I was sent to buy apples, somehow fell into conversation with Willie about books, and was given the run of the library. There was Scott, Dickens, Meredith and Shakespeare, books by Zane Grey and Jeffrey Farnol, and many, many books about the Rocky Mountains. Some person in that nineteenth-century house must have been fascinated by the Rocky Mountains. I didn't differentiate, I read for nothing but pleasure, the way a boy nowadays might watch endless television dramas.

Every week or fortnight, for years, I'd return with five or six books in my oilcloth shopping bag and take five or six away. Nobody gave me direction or advice. There was a tall slender ladder for getting to books on the high shelves. Often, in the incredibly cluttered kitchen, old Willie would ask me about the books over tea and bread. I think it was more out of the need for company than any real curiosity.

I remember one such morning vividly. We were discussing a book I had returned and drinking tea with bread and jam. All I remember about that particular book was that it was large and flat and contained coloured illustrations, of plants and flowers probably, and these would have interested Willie because of the bees. The morning was one of those, still true mornings in summer before the heat comes, the door open on the yard. Earlier that morning he must have gone through his hives – the long grey beard was stained with food and drink and covered his shirt front – and while he was talking some jam fell into the beard and set off an immediate buzzing. Without interrupting the flow of his talk, he shambled to the door, extracted the two or three errant bees caught in the beard, and flung them into the air of the yard.

I continued coming to the house for books after the old beekeeper's death, but there was no longer any talk of books. Andy developed an interest in the land, but, I fear, it was as impractical as astronomy. Because of my constant presence about the house, I was drawn into some of those ventures, but their telling has no place here.

I have often wondered why no curb was put on my reading at home. I can only put it down to a prejudice in favour of the gentle, eccentric Moroneys, and Protestants in general. At the time, Protestants were pitied because they were bound for hell in the next world, and they were considered to be abstemious, honest, and morally more correct than the general run of our fellow Catholics. The prejudice may well have extended to their library. The books may have been thought to be as harmless as their gentle owners. For whatever reason, the books were rarely questioned, and as long as they didn't take from work or prayer I was allowed to read without hindrance.

There are no days more full in childhood than those days that were not lived at all, the days lost in a favourite book. I remember waking out of one such book in the middle of the large living room in the barracks, to find myself surrounded. My sisters had unlaced and removed one of my shoes and placed a straw hat on my head. Only when they began to move the wooden chair on which I sat away from the window did I wake out of the book – to their great merriment.

Nowadays, only when I am writing am I able to find again

that complete absorption when all sense of time is lost, maybe once in a year or two. It is a strange and complete kind of happiness, of looking up from the pages, thinking it is still nine or ten in the morning, to discover that it is past lunchtime; and there is no longer anyone who will test the quality of the absence by unlacing and removing a shoe.

Sometimes I have wondered if it would have made any difference if my reading had been guided or structured, but there is no telling such things in an only life. Pleasure is by no means an infallible, critical guide, W.H. Auden wrote; but it is the least fallible. That library and those two gentle men were, to me, a pure blessing.

A time comes when the way we read has to change drastically or stop, though it may well continue as an indolence or pastime or drug. This change is linked with our growing consciousness, consciousness that we will not live forever and that all human life is essentially in the same fix. We have to discard all the tenets that we have been told until we have succeeded in thinking them out for ourselves. We find that we are no longer reading books for the story and that all stories are more or less the same story; and we begin to come on certain books that act like mirrors. What they reflect is something dangerously close to our own life and the society in which we live.

A new, painful excitement enters the way we read. We search out these books, and these books only, the books that act as mirrors. The quality of the writing becomes more important than the quality of the material out of which the pattern or story is shaped. We find that we can no longer read certain books that once we could not put down; other books that previously were tedious take on a completely new excitement and meaning: even the Rocky Mountains has to become an everywhere, like Mansfield Park, if it is to retain our old affection.

That change happened to me in the Dublin of the 1950s. Again, I think I was lucky. There were many good secondhand book shops in which one could root about for hours. One book barrow in particular, on a corner of Henry Street, was amazing. Most of the books found there then would now be described as modern classics. How the extraordinary Mr Kelly acquired them we never asked. Those were times when books were discussed in dance halls as well as in bars. It was easy then to get a desk in the National Library. The staff were kind and even would bring rare books on request. There were inexpensive seats at the back of the Gate Theatre, and there were many pocket theatres, often in Georgian basements. Out in Dun Laoghaire there was the Gas Company Theatre where we had to walk through the silent showroom of gas cookers to get to see Pirandello or Chekhov or Lorca or Tennesee Williams.

The city was full of cinemas. I remember seeing *Julius Caesar* with Gielgud and Brando playing to full houses in the Metropole. At weekends, cinema tickets were sold on the blackmarket. One such blackmarketeer, a pretty girl I knew, showed me a fistful of unsold tickets one wet Sunday night shortly before eight o'clock and said, 'If I don't get rid of some of these soon – and at bloody cost at that – I'll have to let down me drawers before the night is out'. And there was the tiny Astor on the quays where I first saw *Casque d'Dor*, *Rules of the Game* and *Children of Paradise*.

Much has been written about the collusion of Church and State to bring about an Irish society that was insular, repressive and sectarian. This is partly true, but because of the long emphasis on the local and the individual in a society that never found any true cohesion, it was only superficially successful.

I think that women fared worst of all within this paternalistic mishmash, but to men with intellectual interests it had at the time, I believe, some advantage. Granted, we were young and had very little to lose, but the system was so blatantly foolish in so many of its manifestations that it could only provoke the defence of laughter, though never, then, in public. What developed was a Freemasonry of the intellect with a vigorous underground life of its own that paid scant regard to Church or State. Even an obscene book, we would argue, could not be immoral if it was truly written. Most of the books that were banned, like most books published, were not worth reading, and those that were worth reading could be easily found and quickly passed around. There is no taste so sharp as that of forbidden fruit.

This climate also served to cut out a lot of the pious humbug that often afflicts the arts. Literature was not considered 'good'. There was no easy profit. People who need to read, who need to think and see, will always find a way around a foolish system, and difficulty will only make that instinct stronger, as it serves in another sphere to increase desire. In no way can this clownish system be recommended wholeheartedly, but it was the way it was and we were young and socially unambitious and we managed.

The more we read of other literatures, and the more they

were discussed, the more clearly it emerged that not only was Yeats a very great poet but that almost singlehandedly he had, amazingly, laid down a whole framework in which an indigenous literature could establish traditions and grow. His proud words, 'The knowledge of reality is a secret knowledge; it is a kind of death', was for us, socially as well as metaphorically, true.

The two living writers who meant most to us were Samuel Beckett and Patrick Kavanagh. They belonged to no establishment, and some of their best work was appearing in the little magazines that could be found at the Eblana Bookshop on Grafton Street. Beckett was in Paris. The large, hatted figure of Kavanagh was an inescapable sight around Grafton Street, his hands often clasped behind his back, muttering hoarsely to himself as he passed. Both, through their work, were living, exciting presences in the city. I wish I could open a magazine now with the same excitement with which I once opened *Nimbus*: 'Ignore Power's schismatic sect, / Lovers alone lovers protect'. (The same poet could also rhyme *catharsis* with *arses*, but even his wild swing was like no other.)

When I began to write, and it was in those Dublin years, it was without any thought of publication. In many ways, it was an extension of reading as well as a kind of play. Words had been physical presences for me for a long time before, each word with its own weight, colour, shape, relationship, extending out into a world without end. Change any word in a single sentence and immediately all the other words demand to be rearranged. By writing and rewriting sentences, by moving their words endlessly around, I found that scenes or pictures and echoes and shapes began to emerge that reflected obscurely a world that had found its first expression and recognition through reading. I don't know how long that first excitement lasted – for a few years, I think – before it changed to work, though that first sense of play never quite goes away and in all the most important ways a writer remains a beginner throughout his working life. Now I find I will resort to almost any subterfuge to escape the blank page, but there seems to be always some scene or rhythm that lodges in the mind and will not go away until it is written down. Often when it is written it turns out that there was never anything real behind the rhythm or scene, and it disappears in the writing; other times those scenes or rhythms start to grow, and you find yourself once again working every day, sometimes over a period of several years, to discover and bring to life a world through words as if it were the first and (this is ever a devout prayer) last time. It is true that there can be times of intense happiness throughout the work, when all the words seem, magically, to find their true place, and several hours turn into a single moment; but these occurrences are so rare that they are, I suspect, like mirages in desert fables to encourage and torment the half-deluded traveller.

Like gold in the ground – or the alchemists' mind – it is probably wise not to speak about the pursuit at all. Technique can certainly be learned, and only a fool would try to do without it, but technique for its own sake grows heartless. Unless technique can take us to that clear mirror that is called style, the reflection of personality in language, everything having been removed from it that is not itself, then the most perfect technique is as worthless as mere egotism. Once work reaches that clearness the writer's task is ended. His or her words will not live again until and unless they find their true reader.

JOHN McGAHERN:
A NEW IMAGE?

John Cronin

Since the subject of our symposium is the creative process of the writer, I begin with an episode from John McGahern's short story, 'Peaches', in which we encounter a writer who is confronting that most daunting of creative experiences, writer's block. He sits in a café and opens a letter from his publisher which contains reviews of his last book:

It was never easy to read through reviews, and he read through them quickly when the beer came. It was much as listening to talk about you from another room, and the listener cares little about the quality of the talk as long as it is praise. Always the poor reviews rankled and remained, they were probably nearer the truth in the long run. To publish was to expose oneself naked in an open market, and if the praise was acceptable he could hardly complain of the ridicule, since one always had the choice to stay in original obscurity.[1]

The passage is characterised by McGahern's typically sardonic honesty, which sees both sides of the matter, identifying the writer's very natural sensitivity while also granting the possibility that the poor reviews, even though they rankle, are probably nearer the truth in the long run. Criticism like that contained in such reviews is usually written at a safe distance from its subject but at this symposium at the University of Caen I find myself in the presence of my subject himself. This is a rare, though not unalarming privilege, to find oneself discussing a writer's work with the writer concerned sitting at one's elbow. One has trailed through the Big House, admiring those parts of the building which are open to public gaze and, suddenly, there is the proprietor himself, willing, it seems, to give us access to all those previously roped-off areas and to throw open those closed doors behind which the family has taken refuge from intrusive tourists. It is a heady thought, that one is to be allowed access to the previously unapproachable, even secret places. Later, of course, one comes to realise that the house will continue to hold its secrets. The owner may not wish to reveal all or, indeed, he himself may not have culled all its secrets from the previous occupants. At best, one will come away eventually with new curiosities, new questions.

I have been stumbling about John McGahern's fictional house as an imperceptive tourist for some time, often filled with admiration, sometimes a little puzzled. My occasional encounters with John himself have always been a great personal pleasure, but he has usually been a tactfully reserved cicerone, as is his and every writer's privilege. Called upon now, at short notice, to essay the difficult task of exploring his creative processes, I turn with relief to an insight into his work achieved by another of the symposium's distinguished guests, poet, short story writer, novelist, essayist, that Renaissance man, John Montague. Just over a quarter of a century ago, when just two novels by John McGahern had seen the light, Montague dedicated to him a short poem which memorably encapsulates some important aspects of the writer's genius. I would like to quote it in full:

'A Bright Day'
    for John McGahern

At times I see it, present
As a bright day, or a hill,
The only way of saying something
Luminously as possible.

Not the accumulated richness
Of an old historical language –
That musk-deep odour!
But a slow exactness

Which recreates experience
By ritualizing its details –
Pale web of curtain, width
Of deal table, till all

Takes on a witch-bright glow
And even the clock on the mantel
Moves its hands in a fierce delight
Of so, and so, and so.[2]

This beautifully conveys the peculiar power of the descriptive passages in *The Barracks* and *The Dark*,[3] the two novels which had appeared at the time of the poem's publication. As we read Montague's lines, the living-rooms of those two novels spring vividly to life and we experience again 'the fierce delight of so, and so, and so'. That special kind of participatory pleasure in the actual will be found again in later works by McGahern. One thinks, for example, of the unforgettable account of the morning spent in the schoolyard in the first section of *The Leavetaking*,[4] and the almost unendurable poignancy of the harrowing details of the mother's lonely death. Most recently, *Amongst Women*,[5] his latest novel, in its loving rendering of the Moran farm at Great Meadow, provides welcome evidence that this aspect of the novelist's peculiar power has grown and strengthened over the years. There is no denying his ability to throw 'a witch-bright glow' over ordinary appearances so that they are again and again irradiated into memorable epiphanies. While re-reading many of the short stories in his three collections, *Nightlines, Getting Through* and *High Ground*,[6] I recently noted again his almost pointillist accumulation of detail in his descriptions of place, whether he is tracking his characters through the woods of Oakport or the suburbs of Dublin. In a recent interview with Denis Sampson, he has placed on record his love of words and his sense of their significance:

I think words are things and I think each word has a colour and a personality ... they have a presence outside what they mean ... the pleasure that words give is the comfort of generality – each person lives in his own isolation and out of that the particular is given the grace of ceremony, is given the grace of the general.[7]

This has a Joycean ring to it, recalling the consolatory function ascribed to language by Stephen Dedalus who, in moments of crisis, comforts himself with a phrase such as 'a day of dappled seaborne clouds' as he ponders the mystery of words:

Words, was it their colours? he allowed them to glow and fade, hue after hue: sunrise gold, the russet and green of apple orchards, azure of waves, the grey-fringed fleece of clouds.[8]

McGahern shares Stephen's ambition to mirror an inner world of individual emotions perfectly in a lucid, supple, periodic prose. As a prose writer, he takes his place in a line which extends back through Michael McLaverty to Daniel Corkery. He is, essentially, one of those Irish writers who eschew verbal oddity and high-jinks. Not for him the verbal pyrotechnics of a Carleton or a Flann O'Brien. His grave, plain style deliberately avoids any suggestion of regional quaintness, drawing no attention to itself but working always to render his people and places with vivid fidelity. His fascination with language leads logically to his love of places and their names, a pleasure which he traces to his love of Yeats, that great pronouncer of significant names. In his conversation with Denis Sampson, McGahern recalls his joy in Yeats's naming of places and the delight it gave him to realise that his own well-loved places could stimulate a similar magic:

'To actually see the names like Knocknarea and Queen Maeve's Grave and, you know, "He stood among a crowd at Drumahair / His heart hung all upon a silken dress", to actually know that those place names were places that I knew like Boyle or Carrick-on-Shannon.'[9]

So, McGahern's work familiarises us with a territory which has its special, evocative significance for him and we learn to know Oakport, Boyle and Strandhill as if we had lived in them. His love of and dependence upon his chosen locality recalls the closing lines of Patrick Kavanagh's poem, 'Innocence':

> I cannot die
> Unless I walk outside these whitethorn hedges.[10]

The lines come to mind because McGahern deliberately contrives a kind of fruitfully creative claustrophobia in his work, accustoming us to his people and his places and creating for us a wholly familiar world. As a recent critic has stated:

He is a writer of cycle, of process, of repetition, of 'wheels' as one of his first short stories is called. His medium is not that of change or difference but sameness.[11]

Change, however, was to be attempted after *The Dark*, with peculiarly complicated consequences. He has himself placed on record the creative hiatus which followed on his dismissal from his teaching post in Dublin at the time of the publication of *The Dark*:

'I moved to London. I did some book reviewing. I had temporary jobs, relief teaching, work on the buildings with my brothers-in-law. The usual thing. I grew to love London, but I wasn't able to write. That was the worst part of the sacking. But maybe I wouldn't have written in those years even if there had been no trouble over *The Dark*.'[12]

There is a characteristically self-deprecating modesty about that last remark, a typical unwillingness to enforce too close a causal link between the life and the literature.

The third novel, *The Leavetaking*, saw him making a conscious effort to build upon previous achievement and to advance into new areas of experience which would require of him a radical stylistic experiment. His own brave retrospect sees *The Leavetaking* as a necessary novelty for which he is not prepared to claim complete success, something nevertheless which had to be attempted. 'I would', he told Denis Sampson, 'actually have stopped as a writer unless I had broken out of my own moulds in *The Leavetaking*',[13] and he has gone to considerable lengths to illuminate the special kind of creative struggle on which he embarked in the new novel:

'*The Leavetaking* has two things that have obsessed me all my life, and that's the Self and the Other. That beautiful English word for the Other is Thou. I happen to think that the person cannot emerge from the Self, and that the Other, which is the beloved object, does speak in a different language to the Self. The lyrical language that is used in the first part of the book, which does actually use the refrains of earlier work, and quite consciously so, is almost, in a way, over-lyricised, almost in the direction of verse, so that the language of the Other, which is in the second part of the book, actually should appear as journalese. I think the Self is nothing and that one cannot interpret the Other in the language of the Self. And it's actually why I use pornography in *The Pornographer* because I think that the language of pornography is the opposite language to sexuality and love, that it's an artefact. To interfere with the life of the Other would seem to me to be like bad manners or discourtesy. The life of the Other had to be left there in its own language and that own language is an artefact, and actually its formlessness is a chosen formlessness, so that it's not in itself formlessness. It was something I had to do and I suppose that it cannot be done.'[14]

This lengthy explanation takes its proper place beside the earlier analysis provided by the writer in the Preface to the revised version of *The Leavetaking* which he published in 1984.[15] In that Preface, he describes how the cruel test of translation had revealed to him his dissatisfaction with the second part of that novel as published in 1974. Working through the novel again with its French translator, the poet Alain Delahaye, McGahern became convinced that it must be changed and he undertook a radical revision of part 2 of the novel, considerably reducing it in length. In the Preface to the second edition, the terms 'Self' and 'Other' which he uses in his recent conversation with Denis Sampson, are paralleled by 'I' and 'Otherest':

The Leavetaking was written as a love story, its two parts deliberately different in style. It was an attempt to reflect the purity of feeling with which all the remembered 'I' comes to us, the banal and the precious alike; and yet, how that more than 'I' – the beloved, the 'otherest', the most trusted moments of that life – stumbles continually away from us as poor reportage, and to see if these disparates could in any way be made true to one another.[16]

Later, in the same preface, he describes how he came to see the need for revision of the second part of the novel:

I found myself working through it again with its French translator, the poet Alain Delahaye. The more I saw of it the more sure I was that it had to be changed. The crudity I was attempting to portray, the irredeemable imprisonment of the beloved in reportage, had itself become blatant. I had been too close to the 'Idea', and the work lacked that distance, that inner formality or calm, that all writing, no matter what it is attempting, must possess.[17]

These reflections on his revisionary struggle link *The Leavetaking* with the novel which followed it, *The Pornographer*.[18] McGahern's comments to Denis Sampson on the language of pornography, cited above, establish the link and his frank admission that his tussle with his materials in these two novels was 'something I had to do' leads to the revealing confession, 'I suppose it cannot be done'. In the territory between that necessity and that impossibility the novelist's stylistic struggle is to be observed. Both works are troubled, turbulent, restless. In his latest novel, *Amongst Women*, he has, by contrast, achieved a stylistic seamlessness, a tonal serenity not discernible in either of the two preceding novels. The latest novel possesses to a remarkable degree 'that distance, that inner formality or calm' to which he makes reference in his Preface to the second edition of *The*

Leavetaking. It would seem to be the intense and powerful concentration on the character of Moran which gives *Amongst Women*
its peculiar strength and cohesion. Into that figure, the writer
has fused all the emotional energy that had previously gone to
the fashioning of other father figures in the earlier fiction,
characters such as Reegan in *The Barracks*, Mahoney in *The Dark*,
the father in the short story, 'Korea' or the corresponding patri-
arch in 'Gold Watch'. Moran is the perfection of the type, an
unforgettable combination of paternal autocracy, embittered
nationalism, atavistic piety, twisted love and, probably most of
all, a ruinous fear of life itself. The book's brilliant opening sentence encapsulates with marvellous economy the work's complex
themes of love, hate and fear: 'As he weakened, Moran became
afraid of his daughters'.

The short stories like the novels, manifest an interesting process of development, but where the novelistic maturity represents
a vital stylistic resolution of the struggle between matter and
form, the change in the short stories is, rather, one of mood, from
a cruelly bleak vision of the failure of love to the possibility of
some kind of mutuality. This development can be discerned by
contrasting the first story in *Getting Through*, 'The Beginning of
an Idea', with the last story in *High Ground*, 'Bank Holiday'. The
former is directly relevant to the symposium's theme, since it is
a savage study of the creative process and of its frustration. The
central character, Eva Lindberg, is a successful producer of plays
in an unnamed Scandinavian city. She decides to leave her lover,
Arvo Meri, because he refuses to abandon his wife for her. She
gives up her theatrical career to go to Spain, hoping to write a
story for which she has, literally, 'the beginning of an idea'. The
opening sentence which haunts her mind derives from Chekhov's
short story, 'Oysters' and a detail about Chekhov's burial. In
sunny Spain, she settles down to write but fails completely to do
so. She falls back with relief on translating plays for the theatre
she has left behind. Thus, in the region of the creative, she is a
frustrated failure. In love she is dealt an even crueller hand. The
story, which begins with her worthless lover's failure to commit
himself to her, ends savagely with Eva suffering rape in humili-
ating circumstances by two Spaniards, a fate she brings on herself
by her pseudo-sophisticated interference with their sexual mo-
res. 'The Beginning of an Idea' is an impressive study of love's
most terrible failure, combined with mordant judgements on literary ambition and its inevitable downfall. 'Bank Holiday', on

the other hand, is an altogether more mellow account of successful love and the possibility of marriage between a middle-aged man and an American woman casually introduced to him by a friend. The story's closing sentence offers, in place of the inevitable failure of love so often proffered by McGahern, a vista of unexpected happiness:

They were so tired and happy that it was as if they were already in possession of endless quantities of time and money.[19]

Accustomed to McGahern's normally bleak conclusions, I was surprised by his suddenly producing this uncharacteristically happy ending but my surprise was dissipated when I noted his significant, recent revisions of 'The Image', that somewhat gloomy, artistic manifesto first published in 1968.[20] Revising 'The Image' for the special issue of the *Canadian Journal of Irish Studies* devoted to his work in July, 1991,[21] he made both a telling deletion and an addition which may be of even greater significance. Both changes are worth noting. The deletion comes in the opening sentence of the second paragraph, where the original read:

For art is, out of the failure of love, an attempt to create a world in which we can live . . .[22]

The new version drops the parenthesis and reads:

Art is an attempt to create a world in which we can live . . .[23]

The small but vital addition comes in the closing sentence of the piece. In the first version, this reads:

The Muse, under whose whim we reign, in return for a lifetime of availability, may grant us the absurd crown of style, the 'revelation' in language of this private and unique world each of us possess (*sic*), as we struggle for what may be no more than a yard of lead piping we saw in terror once.[24]

The recent, revised version adds, after 'terror' in the final line, the three telling words, 'or in laughter', thus altering the entire emphasis of the passage, tilting it towards the unexpected possibility of the comic. Thus, art is no longer inextricably tied to love's failure and the human capacity for laughter is newly admitted. This seems a 'New Image', indeed, and one which bodes well for this richly gifted writer in the future.

THE PERSONAE OF SUMMER

John Banville

I do not think I am a novelist. As a writer I have little or no interest in character, plot, motivation, manners, politics, morality, social issues. The word *psychology* when it is applied to art makes me want to reach for my revolver. To those of you who at this point are about to stop reading, let me hasten to say that this is not an anti-humanist attitude I am striking, nor even, really, a postmodernist one. I do believe that the art of fiction does deal with the world, that world which in our arrogance we call 'ordinary', but that it deals with it in very special and specialised ways. I am enough of a deconstructionist to acknowledge that the novelist's intentions for his novel may in the end not count for as much as he imagined or desired that they would. Frequently it happens that a novel will live on into posterity – a rare phenomenon, I grant – because of qualities which for the author were secondary, or of which at the time of writing perhaps he was not even aware. In saying this, however, I do not mean to agree with those critics – and they are by no means only the most advanced ones: read the fiction reviews in the Sunday supplements – who look on the novelist as a dead hand which performs a kind of automatic writing. Novelists themselves contribute to this misconception of what they do and how they do it. When I hear a writer talking earnestly of how the characters in his latest book 'took over the action' I am inclined to laugh (or, if I am in a good mood, acknowledge a colleague doing his best to get through yet another interview). Fictional characters are made of words, not flesh; they do not have free will, they do not exercise volition. They are easily born, and as easily killed off. They have their flickering lives, and die on cue, for us, giving up their little paragraph of pathos. They are t once less and more than what they seem.

The writers I most admire are the ones who have abandoned the pretence of realism, who have ceased to try to speak about things in favour of speaking the things themselves, such as Beckett, or Thomas Bernhard, or those who took the old forms and worked a revolution from within, such as Henry James, or, well, Henry James. The wrought and polished object itself, an astonishment standing in the world – a jar in Tennessee! – that is what interests me. The world and being in it are such a mystery that the artist stands before it in a trance of bafflement, like an idiot at High Mass. In confrontation with the total enigma, all that the artist can do, it seems to me, is set up analogues, parallel microcosms, tiny models of the huge original with which the mind may play in earnest. I am speaking of a pictured world, not a world anatomised. Nietzsche was the first to recognise that the true depth of a thing is in its surface. Art is shallow, and therein lie its deeps. The face is all, and, in front of the face, the mask.

By what means, then, does fiction *get at* the world? Not by engagement, I am convinced, but precisely by disengagement, by adopting a posture of bland innocence, standing back with empty palms on show. Listen, the writer says, listen – here is the music of things as they are, changed upon the blue guitar. The subject matter hardly matters. Flaubert is wondered at and excoriated in equal measure for his stated wish to write a book that would be *about nothing*, but he was merely acknowledging the fact, unpalatable to many, that all art aspires to the condition of pure style. 'In literature,' says Henry James, 'we move through a blest world in which we know nothing except by style, but in which also everything is saved by it.' And here is Theodor Adorno, certainly no proponent of the doctrine of art for art's sake:

The unresolved antagonisms of reality reappear in art in the guise of immanent problems of artistic form. This, and not the deliberate injection of objective moments or social content, defines art's relation to society.

I believe, with Hermann Broch, that art is, or should be, a mode of objective knowledge of the world, not an expression of the subjective world. As Kafka momentously said, the artist is the man who has nothing to say.

....

First comes, for me, the shape. Before I put down even a note for a novel, there exists in my mind, or just outside it somewhere, a figure, not geometrical, exactly, not like something out of Euclid, more a sort of self-sustaining tension in space, tangible yet wholly imaginary, which represents, which in some sense *is*, the completed thing. The task is to bring this figure out of the space of the potential and into the world, where it will be manifest yet hidden, like the skeleton beneath the skin.

At an essential level, therefore, the work of art is for me no more and no less than the solution – partial, always, of course – to a technical problem. The problem is that of placing certain figures on a certain ground so that they shall seem to move, and breathe, and have their lives. How is it to be done? Will it seem paradoxical, in the light of what I have said so far, if I now insist that the only way to portray life in art is to be as lifelike as possible? All that the writer has to work with is human being, his own and that of the mysterious others, what little he can know of it, of them. Even the most abstract art is grounded in the mundane, composed, like us, of Eros and of dust. Life will keep breaking in. However, 'life' here means life in its *appearance*, that is, both in the way it looks, and in the way it makes itself manifest in the world. The phenomenological breath that wafts from that sentence makes me think that the word I should be using in this context is not *life*, but *being*, or even – I whisper it – Being.

The novel, since it is an organic growth, generates, or should, its own rules, which will govern every smallest ramification of its form and content. The novel grows by a process of genetic building, filling itself out, matching itself to its vision of itself, as a tree grows, becoming a tree by becoming a tree. To break the rules of generation is to break the book. Of course, the novelist can make mistakes, and will, since he is human. Randall Jarrell defined the novel as an extended work of prose fiction which has something wrong with it. There are critics who contend that the being wrong – that is, being defective in form, loose in content, ragged in style – is a large part of the novel's strength, that its imperfections make it sturdy and vigorous and lifelike. As Frank Kermode has pointed out, we seek in art a completeness, a 'sense of an ending', not available to us in life (who remembers his own birth, who will know his own death? – all we have is the drifting moment), and, yes, I suppose the truest art will be that which refuses us the neatness of the finished thing. But there is wrong and wrong (there is true and true, also, but that is another matter). Human endeavour can always be counted on for inbuilt flaws, for infelicities of tone and clumsiness of execution. It is when the rules, the deep grammar, of the work of art are bent or broken that the internal structure crumbles. In the novel, such transgressions are more easily detected, I think, than in other forms of art, precisely because the novel is the most lifelike form there is.

Is it not a curious thing, this true-to-lifeness that fiction manages? Albert Einstein was always fascinated, and made not a little uneasy, by the weird way in which physical reality conforms so neatly to the manmade discipline of mathematics. It is hardly less strange that a progression of dark marks on a light surface should cause an eerily persuasive version of the quotidian world to blossom in the brain of the reader sitting under the lamplight with his book, forgetful of himself and of his surroundings. What magic is it that makes us think we are sailing on the Pequod, that we are a little in love with Isabel Archer, that we see the streets of Dublin on a summer day in 1904 through the eyes of Leopold Bloom? How is it that a made-up story should seem to utter that which Wallace Stevens's Large Red Man reads aloud out of the purple tabulae, 'The outlines of being and its expressings, the syllables of its law'? Fiction is a kind of infinitesimal calculus, approaching nearer and ever nearer to life itself and yet never really having anything of real life in it at all, except the fictionist's obsessive and doomed determination to *get it right* (if that really is a human desideratum). Or am I giving too much weight to the merely real?

This is Wallace Stevens again:

> The personae of summer play the characters
> Of an inhuman author, who meditates
> With the gold bugs, in blue meadows, late at night.
> He does not hear his characters talk. He sees
> Them mottled, in the moodiest costumes
>
> Of blue and yellow, sky and sun, belted
> And knotted, sashed and seamed, half pales of red,
> Half pales of green, appropriate habit for
> The huge decorum, the manner of the time,
> Part of the mottled mood of summer's whole,

In which the characters speak because they want
To speak, the fat, the roseate characters,
Free, for a moment, from malice and sudden cry,
Complete in a completed scene, speaking
Their parts as in a youthful happiness.

As always with Stevens, I am not sure that I know what it is
he is talking about here, but I find the passage strangely affect-
ing, and hear in it a description of sorts of what it is I do when I
come to write fiction. The fat, the roseate characters move as in a
moving scene, in this little glass untouchable theatre of the mind.
If they are lifelike it is because so much of life is missing from
them and their doings, the dross which is true life itself thrown
out in obedience to the laws of a necessary economy. Fledgling
novelists are forever worrying about the furniture (how will I
get these characters into bed? – how, for God's sake, will I even
get them up the stairs and through the bedroom door?); it takes
a long time for the apprentice to realise that action in a novel is
not a matter of stage management but of artistic concentration.
Under the artist's humid scrutiny the object grows warm, it stirs
and shies, giving off the blush of verisimilitude; the flash of his
relentless gaze strikes them and the little monsters rise and walk,
their bandages unfurling. The world they inhabit is a world of
words, and yet, as with Josefine the mouse singer's piping song,
'something of our poor brief childhood is in it, something of a
lost happiness that can never be found again, but it also has
something of our busy life here and now, of that little admixture
of unfathomable gaiety which persists and cannot be extin-
guished'. I do not know how it is done. Is it magic or mere
sleight of hand? (Mere?)

IN SEARCH OF THE ROSY GRAIL: THE CREATIVE PROCESS IN THE NOVELS OF JOHN BANVILLE

Rüdiger Imhof

The 'Rosy Grail' is Gabriel Godkin's term to describe the objective of the creative process; it is a symbol of beauty and truth.[1] *Birchwood*, the book in which Gabriel figures and which, in a sense, is his book, presents a lesson in how the creative process operates.

The singularly Proustian Gabriel has set himself the task of telling the story concerning the rise and fall of the Big House Birchwood,[2] thereby trying to come to grips with the nature and truth of his own life. He travels the mad lanes of memory, gathering its *madeleines* and arranging them so as to make them constitute a pattern of sense. The past is a foreign country and Gabriel attempts to discern the whatness of things, the thing-in-itself, like Copernicus and Kepler, in fact all subsequent Banville protagonists: all of them preoccupy themselves with discovering a sublime form of beauty and harmony.

Gabriel is a supreme weaver of words, and *Birchwood* shows him in his efforts to map the past through presenting it in the shape of a narrative. The way Godkin travels is from the Cartesian certainty of 'I am, therefore I think' of the opening to the Wittgensteinian despair of 'whereof I cannot speak, thereof I must be silent' of the end. Gabriel couches his fathoming of the past in a self-conscious, or self-reflexive, form of narrative discourse. The form is self-conscious because its paramount aim is to test how fiction can, or cannot, accommodate life, reality. We observe Banville's main character trying out various narrative genres and conventions in order to explore whether they can do the trick.

In shape, *Birchwood* resembles a clockwork device: wheels-within-wheels, Chinese-box fashion. The wheels are, by and large, constituted by the narrative patterns Gabriel exploits in the course of his *recherche*. There is the big-house genre, the quest romance, or a romantic mystery story with distinctive traits pertaining to the picaresque novel as well as the rationalised Gothic and its offshoots - the tale of ratiocination and the detective novel. Part III, in particular, is very ratiocinatory, assiduously tying up all the loose ends and solving all the carefully planted riddles. The reader, unlike Kepler, can say: 'Everything is told us, and all is explained.' This is the supreme triumph of art, but it is a triumph that has no bearing on reality, as Gabriel himself comes to understand. The withered wizard Prospero has never existed, but Gabriel wanted to keep him, 'with his cloak and his black hat', and so he 'became [his] own Prospero, and [ours]' (*B*, p. 168) - a magician, a wizard with words.

Birchwood is, in the final analysis, about the literary, or artistic, imagination and about how the artistic imagination tries to come to terms with the world, life, truth - a thematic concern that is, notably enough, of the utmost significance for *The Book of Evidence*. Gabriel has, just like that paradigmatic magician Prospero, conjured up a world. He has tried out a wide variety of different literary genres, conventions and stereotypes to see whether these could assist him in his quest for perfection, to see whether they could help discover 'a form which could contain and order all [his] losses' (*B*, p. 171). But the conventions and strategies did not stand up to the task. All they were suited for was to be parodied, in order that their exhausted nature may be discerned. At the end Gabriel resigns himself to the fact that there 'is no form, no order, only echoes, coincidences, sleight of hand, dark laughter. I accept it.' (*B*, p. 171) He has failed because the old forms were of no use to him and new, more adequate ones he has as yet not been able to discover. He has also failed because each and every artistic effort to arrive at perfection can at best be an approximation. The rosy grail forever eludes the artist's grasp. As Cecil Day Lewis, referring to a statement by T.S. Eliot, has put it: '[. . .] every new poem is [. . .] a new start; and at best it is but a tolerable substitute for the poem no one is ever great enough to write.'[3] In a way, all of Banville's novels to date present instructive cases of failure.

Gabriel Godkin's forerunner is Ben White, in *Nightspawn*. He, too, is seeking to ascertain how 'time [can] be vanquished'

(*N*, p. 107) in the 'sinister pages' of the book he is presenting to his reader. He, too, is 'talking about the past, about remembrance [. . .], about Mnemosyne, that lying whore' (*N*, p. 113); and like Godkin, he is essentially talking about art, as he admits at the end of his account (*N*, p. 224).

Ostensibly, *Nightspawn is* concerned with a *coup d'état* in Greece, telling of how White got entangled in the events. The novel masquerades as a thriller, with all the customary para-phernalia of the genre. And yet, *Nightspawn is* anything but an ordinary thriller: the book is a metafiction that deliberately wears the conventions on its sleeve. 'I open the box and there it is, an image cut from jewels, and quivering between the azure lid and bed of sapphire silk' (*N*, p. 7), Ben White remarks near the open-ing. He is cast in the role of a novelist who opens his box of tricks and conjures up a self-sufficient world.

Nightspawn is replete with self-conscious metafictional re-marks, intertextual references as well as instances of a parodic turning-inside-out of generic strategies and essential ingredients of thrillers. They are too numerous and conspicuous to escape one's attention. His creative efforts land Ben White in an artistic predicament that has come to be associated with the narratorial voices in Beckett, especially those of the trilogy.

Like many a Beckett narrator, Ben White urges himself on, while at the same time admitting his impotence: 'He blundered about the room. I cannot go on. I watched him. On, on, you cunt.' (*N*, p. 209) In the very last section of the novel, he is compelled to acknowledge that his efforts to transfix a period in his life have been born out of a desire to escape the 'suffocating void' (*N*, p. 223) of silence, which will engulf him as soon as he has set down the last word. Therefore he makes his words go on and on 'until we are all up to our balls in paper' (*N*, p. 224) – a situation also evoked at the end of Nabokov's *Bend Sinister*. Tell-ing stories is being alive, but they should be stories that have no other pretensions than to be artifice. As soon as they attempt to transfix, or represent, reality, 'to express it all' (*N*, p. 224), they are bound to fail. This is the final lesson Ben White is constrained to learn.

There is one character in the book who holds an extraordi-nary attraction for White. His name is Yacinth. He serves as a personification of Beauty. The boy is on two occasions associated with 'a single red rose' (*N*, pp. 87, 117), and he prefigures Godkin's 'rosy grail' . Ben, at one point, recalls with great vividness how

Yacinth had stood on the landing in the grey dawn hour and
bared his teeth at him (*N*, p. 132), and he thinks some revelation
was offered him there. Later, he sees the boy bent over a paper,

writing swiftly, smiling, with that smile, so perfect, so absorbed, a thing
which seemed to exist, like himself, like music, without reference to
anything else in the world. (*N*, p. 200)

Then Ben accidentally kills the boy, bemoaning his loss:
'Yacinth, my Hyacinth' (*N*, p. 212). Thumbing through the 'file
against humanity' of his friend, Eric, he comes across this entry:
'*What the heart desires, the world is incapable of giving*' (*N*, p. 214).
As he is an artist, a writer, his heart desires truth and beauty, but
the world is incapable of giving him the means to preserve truth
and transfix beauty once and for all. Yacinth bares his teeth at
him; beauty defies the artist. And in the end the artist kills beauty
through his necessarily inadequate efforts.

Beauty and the quest for harmony and order also defy
Banville's scientists. Copernicus and Kepler are obsessed, just as
artists are, with order and harmony, with discovering the Kantian
thing itself, the vivid thing. When Andreas, Copernicus's brother
and *alter ego*, sums up the fruits of all that star-gazing in
Copernicus's last hallucinatory vision, he says that Copernicus
'thought to discern the thing itself, the eternal truths, the pure
forms that lie behind the chaos of the world' (*C*, p. 238). 'You
looked into the sky' , he goes on; 'what did you see?' , he asks. 'I
saw...the planets dancing, and heard them singing in their courses'
(*C*, p. 238), Copernicus replies, and Andreas counters:

O no, no brother. These things you imagined. Let me tell you how it
was. You set the sights of the triquetrum upon a light shining in the sky,
believing that you thus beheld a fragment of reality, inviolate, unmis-
takable, enduring, but that was not the case. What you saw was a *light
shining in the sky*; whatever it was more than that it was so only by
virtue of your faith, your belief in the possibility of apprehending reality. (*C*, pp. 238f.)

Another failure, then, like Kepler after him, who also heard
the planets sing in their courses and produce music of heavenly
harmony, as he tried to argue in his *Harmonice mundi*, where he
sought to build the universe around 'that great five-note chord
from which the world's music is made' (*K*, p. 48).

But Banville's Copernicus and Kepler are artist-figures not

only as a result of their preoccupation with truth, beauty, harmony and order, of their search for the rosy grail. Additionally, they are shown to make their revolutionary discoveries much as artists do with regard to their artefacts: the scientific process of physical investigation is likened by Banville to the creative process. Copernicus and Kepler arrive at their findings through intuition and the power of imagination, rather than by dint of fastidious drudgery and heart-rending exertion. The latter lands Kepler only in a maze of mistakes and contradictions. It is only when he feels great wings brushing against him, perhaps the wings of the Angel of Annunciation, another Gabriel alongside Godkin and Swan, that he hits upon the solution to the problem of the world harmony.

When the solution came, it came, as always, through the back door of the mind, hesitating shyly, an announcing angel dazed by the immensity of the journey. (*K*, p. 182)

Similarly, Copernicus comes by the solution to the cosmic mystery by chance, inspiration and intuition: when least expected.

And then at last it came to him, sauntered up behind him, as it were, humming happily, and tapped him on the shoulder, wanting to know the cause of all the uproar. [. . .] it came [. . .] like a magnificent great slow golden bird alighting in his head with a thrumming of vast wings. (*C*, p. 84)

Copernicus's supreme fiction is the consequence, significantly, of 'a creative leap' (*C*, p. 85). He treats the solution as if he were an artist, a sculptor, say, marvelling at the beauty of his finished work and deriving an immense aesthetic pleasure from it.

He turned the solution this way and that, admiring it, as if he were turning in his fingers a flawless ravishing jewel. It was the thing itself, the vivid thing. (*C*, p. 85)

Copernicus's labours, like the incessant efforts of a creative artist, are described as 'a progress of progressive failure' (*C*, p. 93). His book is 'not science – it is a dream' (*C*, p. 207). Kepler will entitle one of his books 'Somnium' : a dream bodying forth the perennial dream of the artist to be able to coerce the chaos that is the world into some harmonious whole.

Finally, Copernicus and Kepler are artist-figures because their creative efforts, notably enough, result in supreme fictions:

unifying systems of magnificent harmony and beauty that, alas, have no counterpart in reality – just as with works of art. Incidentally, Kepler's model of the universe centred around the five Platonic solids could be compared with an artefact, is in fact one.

Part of the reason why the astronomers fail is that they have to rely on language to communicate their discoveries, whether these be supreme fictions or not. Copernicus confronts that problem early on, when – much like Stephen Dedalus – he becomes aware that words are but arbitrary signs for things and ideas. 'Tree. That was its name', young Copernicus reflects about the thing he sees outside the window of his room:

And also: linden. They were nice words. He had known them a long time before he knew what they meant. They did not mean themselves, they were nothing in themselves, they meant the dancing thing outside. In wind, in silence, at night, in the changing air, it changed and yet was changelessly the tree, the linden tree. That was strange. (*C*, p. 3)

Before he dies, Copernicus imagines his brother, Andreas, telling him: 'We say only those things that we have the words to express: it is enough.' (*C*, p. 240) It was Rilke who, in the ninth elegy of *Duino Elegies*, defined the task of the artist in these terms:

> [. . .] are we, perhaps, *here* just for saying: House.
> Bridge, Fountain, Gate, Jug, Fruit tree, Window, –
> Possibly: Pillar, Tower? . . . But for *saying*, remember,
> Oh, for such saying as never the things themselves
> Hoped so intensely to be.[4]

Copernicus set out to say the things as never the things themselves hoped so intensely to be. But near the end of his life, he feels forced to acknowledge that he has failed, has had to fail, in no small measure because of his lacking the necessary linguistic resources for conveying truth. Language, that inexorable falsifier, interposed itself between the vivid thing and his efforts at saying, in Rilke's sense.

The historian in *The Newton Letter* encounters comparable problems with words. These are problems as expressed by Hugo von Hofmannsthal's Lord Chandos.[5] We shall forbear to treat in any detail here of how Banville's Newton biographer, ensconced in the lodge of Fern somewhere in the south of Ireland, dreams up a horrid drama about the people he comes to know during his stay and fails to see the commonplace tragedy that is playing itself out in real life (*NL*, cf. p. 79). His is a case of reality perceived through a somewhat crooked, or tainted, imagination. We may forego a detailed consideration, since such questions as may be posed in connection with *The Newton Letter* and its idiosyncratic main character can, in a sense, more profitably be raised in a discussion of *The Book of Evidence, so* far quite copiously commented on and fulsomely praised, mostly for the wrong reasons.

First, however, and mainly to complete the picture, we will allow a brief look at *Mefisto*. Gabriel Swan is an artist-figure not only in the sense in which Copernicus and Kepler are seen as artist-figures. He is presented in his endeavour to make sense of his life by accounting for it in the form of a sustained narrative, and by imposing upon his account a very specific design. That design has two noteworthy aspects to it. First, it follows Joyce's method of basing a narrative on a literary precedent, primarily Goethe's *Faust*. Second, it imbues this compositional approach with a sense of order of its very own.

Swan is as much concerned with the chaos of the world as Copernicus and Kepler. '[. . .] under the chaos of things a hidden order endures' (*M*, p. 211), he contends. Whereas Kepler thought in terms of geometrical patterns, Gabriel's epistemological tools are figures. They are, or rather, 'were [his] friends' (*M*, p. 31), providing the foundation on which he meant to erect his system of the world, before his experience with Felix and above all with Kosok and his Dante-esque computer laboratory began to shatter and finally broke down his conviction. At the end, he acquiesces in the notion that everything is governed by chance. But the concept of chance that Gabriel Swan eventually comes to embrace only *appears* to be negativistic. For ultimately he does not relinquish his faith in order. Chance does not mean complete randomness for Gabriel, and the specific nature of his concept becomes manifest through the particular shape of his autobiographical narrative.

Mefisto is grounded on a palindromic design, as hinted by the opening paragraph; binary patterns and mirror-symmetrical arrangements abound. For instance, Part II is a near-replica of Part I, as far as events and character-constellations go. The question is, of course, why Gabriel, or for that matter Banville, should have taken so much trouble to impose such a concept of order. An answer can be given with reference to Democritus's atomistic world view, Nietzsche's 'die ewige Wiederkunft' , 'fractals' and contemporary chaos theory.[6] Furthermore, principles of duality would seem to be the most appropriate ordering devices in an attempt to come to terms with the essential nature of the world because the phenomena that go to make up the world are largely built on the principle of duality, symmetry and palindromic patterns.[7] The form of *Mefisto*, thus, bodies forth the order, harmony, symmetry and completeness underlying the seemingly contingent world of Gabriel's near-Faustian experiences in a Mephistophelian world.

Gabriel is yet another supreme weaver of fictions, like his namesake Gabriel in *Birchwood*. Near the end, he admits to having lost Kasperl's black notebook, but he consoles himself and the reader by pointing out: 'Have I not made a black book of my own?' (*M*, p. 233) It is the book that the reader is just about to finish reading: *Mefisto*, which in its original edition was bound in black covers. Only now, at the close, when everything is almost done, does the reader become fully aware that he has borne witness to a sly and subtle act of artistic, or narrative, creation. He has, as it were, peered over the artist's shoulder, while that wizard with words was imposing order where chaos appeared to hold sway, or while yet another Prospero-figure was engaged in a creative process - incidentally just as is the case at the end of Proust's *A la recherche*, where there is another Swan, albeit with two n's.

Mefisto depicts a Mephistophelian, or rather a Nietzschean world in which God has absconded, or possibly even died. Ethical and moral principles are turned topsy-turvy. The world of *The Book of Evidence is* an extension of the Nietzschean ideas informing *Mefisto*, in particular those advanced by Nietzsche regarding notions of morality and ethics. The novel probes a moral issue. What use are concepts of good and evil? '*Have the adherents of the theory of free-will the right to punish?*' , asks Nietzsche,[8] and he concludes that they '*have no right*' to punish.[9] Freddie Montgomery argues:

I wish to claim full responsibility for my actions [. . .] and I declare in advance that I shall accept without demur the verdict of the court. I am merely asking, with all respect, whether it is feasible to hold on to the principle of moral culpability once the notion of free will has been abandoned. (*BE*, p. 16)

This is just one example that may prove Nietzsche's influence. Another may be found in this quotation from *Human, All Too Human*:

Man's complete lack of responsibility for his behaviour, and for his nature, is the bitterest drop which the man of knowledge must swallow if he had been in the habit of seeing responsibility and duty as humanity's claim to nobility. All his judgements, distinctions, dislikes have thereby become worthless and wrong: the deepest feeling he had offered a victim or a hero was misdirected; he may no longer praise, no longer blame, for it is nonsensical to praise and blame nature and necessity. Just as he loves a work of art, but does not praise it, just as he regards a plant, so he must see the actions of men and his own actions.[10]

The *Book of Evidence* looks like a simple, straightforward novel: it does not seem to be as 'bookish' as the rest of Banville's work to date. But in Banville, as in life, nothing is quite that simple or straightforward. Like *Nightspawn, Birchwood, The Newton Letter,* and *Mefisto, The Book of Evidence* essentially probes the relationship between art and life, portraying its narrator-protagonist in the act of artistic creation. In the final analysis, the novel offers a self-reflexive and self-reflective approach to a specific form of poetic sensibility.

Comparison has been drawn between Banville's novel and Wilde's *De Profundis*, Sartre's *La Chute,* and Gide's *L'Immoraliste*.[11] The most obvious parallel, though, has so far escaped those who have analysed the book. Banville's greatest indebtedness is to the Nabokov of *Lolita*, itself a 'book of evidence'. *The Book of Evidence is* only on the surface about a senseless murder and the murderer's efforts to justify his behaviour, just as *Lolita is* only on the most accessible level a narrative dealing with a nymphet, one man's passionate love for her and a panoramic journey across the United States. In essence, both books are about art.

Throughout *Lolita*, Humbert can be observed manipulating the averred facts of life through art, or literature, as when he compares Lolita to Carmen:

O my Carmen, my little Carmen, something, something, those something nights, and the stars, and the cars, and the bars, and the barmen [. . .][12]

Like Freddie in so many cases, Humbert is thereby provoking the reader to view the events in his life in terms of a literary precedent – the Carmen situation. He is surreptitiously laying a trap, arousing distinctive expectations, but then deliberately thwarting them. At one point, Humbert notes: 'As greater authors than I have put it: "Let readers imagine"', but he tellingly

continues: 'On second thought, I may as well give those imagi-
nations a kick in the pants' (*L*, p. 67). Most of *Lolita* consists of a
linguistic-cum-literary game. 'Darling, this is only a game' ,
Humbert pleads(*L*, p. 22). Little wonder that he should begin his
story thus:

Lolita, light of my life, fire of my loins. My sin, my soul. Lo-lee-ta: the
tip of the tongue taking a trip of three steps down the palate to tap, at
three, on the teeth. (*L*, p. 11)

For he self-reflexively remarks: 'You can always count on a murderer for a fancy prose style' (*L*, p. 11). That fancy prose style, as
fancy as Freddie's in every respect, throws into relief right at the
very start that what the reader confronts is a linguistic construct
– letters and words on a number of pages. Freddie, in turn,
opens his account in these terms: 'My Lord, when you ask me to
tell the court in my own words, this is what I shall say' (*BE*, p.3),
thereby putting special emphasis on the primacy of text, on the
verbal nature of what follows. No less unequivocally, Humbert
states: 'Oh, my Lolita, I have only words to play with!' (*L*, p. 34)
And play with them he most certainly does, Humbert Humbert,
whose name echoes that of the car which Freddie rents: an old
Humber, which he finds at a garage called 'Melmoth's Car Hire'
(*BE* p. 90) – an allusion that intimates the wanderings (both
physical and spiritual) of Freddie as well as a nod to Humbert's
own automobile: a 'Dream Blue Melmoth' (*L*, p. 229) and
Humbert's reference to it at the end of *Lolita:* 'Hi, Melmoth, thanks
a lot, old fellow' (*L*, p. 309).

When Humbert remarks about himself:

When I try to analyse my own cravings, motives, actions and so forth, I
surrender to a sort of retrospective imagination which feeds the analytic
faculty with boundless alternatives and which causes each visualized
route to fork and re-fork without end in the maddeningly complex
prospect of my past. (*L*, p. 15)

he characterises Freddie Montgomery's situation in an unwit-
tingly precise manner. Humbert's imagination invents nymphets,
constructs a similarity between Humbert's love for Lolita and
Dante's love for Beatrice (*L* p. 21). Again life is viewed through
literature. Later he enters his name as 'Mr. Edgar H. Humbert
(I threw in the 'Edgar' just for the heck of it)' (*L*, p. 77). That
'Edgar' refers to none other than Edgar Allan Poe, another liter-

ary precedent. Freddie, signing a document in the garage where he hires the car in the name of Smyth, thinks 'the *y* a fiendishly clever touch' (*BE*, p. 99). Humbert also admits to 'degrading and dangerous desires' (*L*, p. 26), to his 'criminal craving' (*L*, p. 25), just as Freddie will after him. And like Freddie, Humbert is 'an artist and a madman' (*L*, p. 19).

Lolita is about the notion of man as an essentially and invisibly caged animal; but even more so, it is about art itself as a kind of beautiful caging. Nabokov's impulse seems to have been to create a portrait of a man imprisoned in passion, like the ape who is referred to in the text as having drawn the bars of his cage from the inside. Humbert is the prisoner of his past, in particular his idyllic and brutally disrupted childhood romance, which, significantly, he sees in terms of Poe's 'Annabel Lee' poem. Nabokov's method, just as Banville's, is an intertextual one, with allusions and references to Poe, Mérimée, Proust, Dostoevsky, Dante, Sherlock Holmes and myriad other writers, in addition to allusions to, and exploitations of, literary conventions.

Lolita purports to be a book written by Humbert Humbert in order to eternalise his love and externalise his pain, his *Dolores*, Lolita's real first name. Yet, the Lolita he writes about is not a real person, never was one for Humbert, like the maid never was for Freddie. Lolita is only a figment, a product of Humbert's imagination whose consummation he undertook for aesthetic purposes: to satisfy his sense of beauty. The act of love, for Humbert, equals an act of satisfying his sense of beauty. Humbert is an aesthete; however, his aesthetic attitude lacks humanness, at least for the most part. Freddie is Humbert's kith and kin.

Lolita could be read as a lesson in the potential inhumanity of the kind of aesthetic attitude that fails to have moral commitment. This is also the way in which *The Book of Evidence* could, or rather can, be read. In the end, Humbert comes to acknowledge that such commitment is of the essence. The last scene showing him and Lolita together make his point by evincing how closely Lolita is committed to her husband and her child.

The foregoing comparative comments may appear to make up rather an inordinately digressive excursus; yet, by way of analogy, they have a close bearing on The *Book of Evidence,* outlining the novel's thematic *raison d'être*. In more concrete terms, while Banville's other high, cold heroes – from Canon Koppernigk to Gabriel Swan – did not contract to be known and forfeited their humaneness and human happiness by staying aloof from

life, Freddie Montgomery, at one point equally about to become
'one of those great, cold technicians, the secret masters of the
world' (*BE*, p. 65) with his proficiency in statistics and probabil-
ity theory (*BE*, p. 18)[13] as a means of making 'the lack of certainty'
in the world, 'an unpredictable, seething world [. . .] a swirl of
chance collisions' (*BE*, p. 18) more manageable – Freddie, then,
gets horrifyingly involved, and horrifyingly involves himself,
in the business of the world; and the irony of it all is that he,
too, is deprived of his humaneness, ending up in jail for a most
cold-blooded murder. 'When you have once seen the chaos',
Copernicus says,

> you must make something to set between yourself and that terrible
> sight; and so you make a mirror, thinking that in it shall be reflected the
> reality of the world; but then you understand that the mirror reflects
> only appearances, and that reality is somewhere else, off behind the
> mirror; and then you remember that behind the mirror there is only
> chaos. (*C* p. 209)

It is an utterly apt description of what Freddie does in 'real' life
as well as in and *through* his 'book of evidence'. Freddie's mirror
is art.

After the bottom has fallen out of his world, his pursuit is
seen as a desire arising from the disjunction experienced between reality and the imagination's attempt to grasp it. 'What a
surprise the familiar always is' (*BE*, p. 40), Freddie notes, thus
echoing the epistemological predicament of the historian in *The
Newton Letter*. Copernicus looked at the sky and he saw the stars;
they bore him upwards in a state of sublime bliss; however, they
failed to make sense, or rather not in the way in which the
ancients had tried to account for them – *salvare phenomena* and
all. As a consequence, he strove towards reading sense into them,
setting up a theory that would explain the phenomena, rather
than simply save them. Although he came quite close to the
truth, his concept of the cosmos ultimately remained a supreme
fiction. Kepler, too, looked at the sky and perceived the stars and
the planets; he heard them produce a music of divine harmony,
but he likewise could make little of them, the chaos of the cosmos defying most of his efforts. Similarly, the Newton historian
and Gabriel Swan yield their epistemological efforts to appearances and chance, respectively. And Freddie commits a senseless
murder and subsequently attempts to make sense of a senseless
crime. The outcome is, no less, a supreme fiction – Freddie's

very own 'book of evidence'. That book, though, has a slightly sinister side to it, in that it shifts the task of establishing sense onto the reader. Freddie slyly manoeuvres the reader into a situation where he finds himself seeking to make sense of a senseless attempt at justifying a senseless deed.

Notably enough, Freddie presents the events of his narrative framed, or caged, by literature, film or works of art. A considerable number of such scenes are rendered as if they were animated extant pictures and paintings. For instance, the scene where Freddie, for the first time, enters the room with wallpaper the colour of tarnished gold and thinks he has 'stepped straight into the eighteenth century' (*BE*, p. 77), that room in which he finds the painting, entitled *Portrait of a Woman with Gloves*,[14] is done in terms of a description of Balthus' painting 'The Room'. The films alluded to include *White Heat, Blue Velvet*, and *Aguirre – Der Zorn Gottes*. Literary references are, for instance, to *Ulysses* (*BE*, p. 37), *Oedipus* Rex (*BE*, p. 30) and, of course, to *Lolita*. Mention is made of the names of Van Gogh, Hogarth, Jan Steen, and Lautrec. As one who is inexorably turning away from the reality of life towards a fictive unreality, the confessing Freddie must create a supreme fiction to lend credence to his past, a past which itself had 'all seemed no more than a vivid fiction' (*BE*, p. 150).

In the novel, there is a definite development from an initial 'nothing' in a doorway (*BE*, p. 159) to an 'invisible presence' (*BE*, p. 204) and a final recognition of what this door-frame should usher forth: 'a child, a girl, one whom I will recognise at once, without the shadow of a doubt' (*BE*, p. 219). This desire to give life is ironically coloured by the prospect of Freddie's probable sentence – life. The child, Freddie is condemned to create on 'the blank inner wall' (*BE*, p. 72) of his heart, as he once failed to do with his wife.[15]

Briefly, the idea informing this creative urge seems to be this: Freddie names his 'essential sin [. . .], the one for which there will be no forgiveness' (*BE*, p. 215) as a 'failure of imagination'. He never imagined Josie Bell 'vividly enough, [. . .] never made her be there sufficiently' (*BE*, p. 215): he did not make her 'live' Whether it is a telling case of class-consciousness or not,[16] Freddie can see Anna Behrens in terms of the Dutch masters, and his mother as one of 'Lautrec's ruined doxies' (*BE*, p. 59), or is able to evoke an extensive and empathic scene of how the woman in the painting was portrayed, but cannot adequately picture the maid's world; in fact, the only descriptive details he notes down about the maid concern her 'extraordinary pale, violet eyes' (*BE*, p. 111), 'her mousy hair and bad skin, that bruised look around her eyes' (BE, p. 113): that is all the reader learns of her. Freddie killed Josie because he could kill her, and he could kill her because for him she was not alive. His task now, he pre-eminently feels, is

to bring her back to life. I am not sure what that means, but it strikes me with the force of an unavoidable imperative. How am I to make it come about, this act of parturition? (*BE*, pp. 215f.)

The answer is that Freddie effects this act of parturition by caging Josie in a work of art, by capturing part of her life and his own involvement in it, but even more so her death in a full-fledged narrative – a book of evidence, art.

Freddie's redemption, if redemption it is, lies in an acknowledgement of the disjunction that exists between the artistic and the 'commonplace world' (*BE*, p. 108) and the impossibility of ever bridging such a gap. Through his confession, Freddie relives the words of Humbert Humbert, who admits that the only amends he can make to his victim is 'transfiguration in a work of art'. He develops from his former ignorance to an understanding of the schism between the real and the imaginary and accepts the despair inherent in this equation.[17]

In a way, all of Banville's novels are a celebration of the beauty of our brief lives. Every so often Freddie Montgomery is unexpectedly struck by that beauty, which he inevitably discovers in the commonplace. In that sense, even in Freddie – as Banville has suggested[18] – there is such a celebration, if only in that he, Freddie, succeeds in bringing forth a supreme fiction in a creative process that may bring to mind Rilke's description of how an artist creates, in *Malte Laurids Brigge*:

But one must also have been beside the dying, must have sat beside the dead in a room with open windows and fitful noises. And still it is not yet enough to have memories. One must be able to forget them when they are many and one must have immense patience to wait until they come again. For it is the memories themselves that matter. Only when they have turned to blood within us, to glance and gesture, nameless and no longer to be distinguished from ourselves only then can it happen that in a most rare hour the first word of a poem arises in their midst and goes forth from them.[19]

NOTES

NOTES

SEAMUS HEANEY AND THE GENTLE FLAME

Maurice Harmon

1. *Irish Times*, 14 November 1974.
2. *New York Times Magazine*, 13 March 1983.
3. *Irish Tribune*, 30 September 1984.
4. I have dealt with this in 'We Pine for Ceremony: Ritual and Reality in the Poetry of Seamus Heaney (1965-1975)', *Studies on Seamus Heaney*, ed. by Jacqueline Genet. Caen: Centre de Publications de l'Université de Caen, 1987, pp. 47-64. Reprinted in *Seamus Heaney: A Collection of Critical Essays*, ed. by Elmer Andrews. Basingstoke: Macmillan, 1992.
5. See his essay, 'The Placeless Heaven: Another Look at Kavanagh', in *The Government of the Tongue*. London: Faber & Faber, 1988, pp. 3-14.

JOHN MONTAGUE: PASSIONATE CONTEMPLATIVE

Augustine Martin

1. Following C.S. Lewis in *The Four Loves*, London: Geoffrey Bles Ltd, 1960, I call sexual love *eros*, family love *affection*, divine love *agape*, non-sexual love between people of the same sex *friendship*.
2. Dillon Johnston is an exception: in his illuminating book, *Irish Poetry After Joyce*, Notre Dame/Dolmen 1985, he devotes several pages to this aspect of Montague's work.
3. 'To the Rose upon the Rood of Time', *Collected Poems of W.B. Yeats*.
4. *The Lost Notebook* by John Montague, Dublin/Cork: The Mercier Press, 1987.
5. The sea imagery of 'Anchor' tempts one to refer also to an equally pervasive Catholic hymn which begins

   Hail Queen of Heaven, the ocean star,
   Guide of the wanderer here below.'
   Thrown on life's surge, we claim thy care
   Save us from peril, and from woe.
   Virgin most pure, Star of the Sea
   Pray for the wanderer, pray for me.

In the shadow of the Stella Maris church, Sandymount, that intrepid voyager, Leopold Bloom, consummated his 'long and seafed silent rut'.

6. A trenchant analysis of the politico-historical implications of Montague's poetry is to be found in Gerald Dawe's 'Invoking the Powers' in *Chosen Ground*, edited by Neil Corcoran, Seren Press, University of Wales, 1992.

7. During the Easter ceremonies the priest, in the old Latin Rite would instruct the congregation 'Flectamus genua!', 'Kneel down!' followed by 'Levate!', 'Rise up!'

THOMAS KILROY'S WORLD ELSEWHERE

Christopher Murray

Acknowledgement is made to *Éire – Ireland* and to the Irish American Cultural Institute of St Paul, Minnesota, for permission to print this article.

1. See Anthony Roche, 'Thomas Kilroy', in *Post-War Literatures in English*, Groningen: Wolters-Noordhoff, 1989, pp. 1-13; Denis Sampson, 'The Theatre of Thomas Kilroy: Boxes of Words', in *Perspectives of Irish Drama and Theatre*, eds. Jacqueline Genet and Richard Allen Cave, Gerrards Cross: Colin Smythe, 1991, pp. 130-39; Barbara Hayley, 'Self-Denial and Self-Assertion in Some Plays of Thomas Kilroy: *The Madame MacAdam Travelling Theatre*,' in *Studies on the Contemporary Irish Theatre*, eds. Jacqueline Genet and Elisabeth Hellegouarc'h, Caen: Université de Caen, 1991, pp. 47-56. An exception, in being specifically focussed, is the critique by Michael Etherton in *Contemporary Irish Dramatists*, Houndmills, Basingstoke: Macmillan, 1989, pp. 51-62.

2. Malcolm Bradbury and James McFarlane (eds.), *Modernism 1890-1930*, Harmondsworth: Penguin, 1976, p. 26.

3. *Ibid.*, p. 27.

4. Katharine Worth places greater emphasis on the symbolist tradition, in *The Irish Drama of Europe from Yeats to Beckett*, London: Athlone Press, 1978.

5. W.B. Yeats, *Essays and Introductions*, London: Macmillan, 1961, p. 224.

6. W.B. Yeats, *Autobiographies*, London: Macmillan, 1961, p. 279.

7. Raymond Williams, *Drama from Ibsen to Brecht*, Harmondsworth: Penguin, 1973, p. 7.

8. Thomas Kilroy, 'The Irish Writer: Self and Society, 1950-80', in *Literature and the Changing Ireland*, ed. Peter Connolly, Gerrards Cross: Colin Smythe; Totowa, NJ: Barnes & Noble, 1982, p. 181.

9. Samuel Beckett, 'Recent Irish Poetry', in *Disjecta Membra*, ed. Ruby Cohn, London: Calder, 1983, p. 70.

10. Sean O'Faolain, '1916-1941: Tradition and Creation', in *The Bell*, 11, April 1941, p. 6.
11. See Irving Wardle, *The Theatres of George Devine*, London: Jonathan Cape, 1978.
12. See Alan Simpson, *Beckett and Behan and a Theatre in Dublin*, London: Routledge and Kegan Paul, 1962.
13. Thomas Kilroy, 'Groundwork for an Irish Theatre', in *Studies*, XLVIII, 1959, p. 198. Kilroy directly praised George Devine and the Royal Court model on p. 197. See also Gerald Dawe, 'Thomas Kilroy', in *Theatre Ireland*, 3, June/September, 1983, p.117.
14. Sean O'Faolain, *op. cit.*, p. 10.
15. Edward Albee, *Who's Afraid of Virginia Woolf?*, Harmondsworth: Penguin, 1965, pp. 29-30, 70-71.
16. Thomas Kilroy, *The Death and Resurrection of Mr Roche*, London; Faber and Faber, 1969, p. 18.
17. Thomas Kilroy, 'A Generation of Playwrights', *Irish University Review*, 22, 1992, p. 137.
18. Thomas Kilroy, 'Two Playwrights: Yeats and Beckett', in *Myth and Reality in Irish Literature*, ed. Joseph Ronsley, Waterloo, Ontario: Wilfrid Laurier University Press, 1977, p. 185.
19. Thomas Kilroy, '*The Moon in the Yellow River*: Denis Johnston's Shavianism', in *Denis Johnston: A Retrospective*, ed. Joseph Ronsley, Gerrards Cross: Colin Smythe; Totowa, NJ: Barnes & Noble, 1981, pp. 49-58.
20. Thomas Kilroy, 'Two Playwrights: Yeats and Beckett', *op. cit.*, p. 37.
21. Thomas Kilroy, *Talbot's Box*, Dublin: Gallery Press, 1979, p. 63. Cf. the stage direction for Talbot's resurrection, p. 19, which calls for 'blinding beams of light' and a 'high-pitched wailing cry' which must be 'of physical discomfort to the audience'.
22. *Ibid.*, p. 47. Cf. Kilroy's Fr. Lanigan in *The Big Chapel*, London: Faber and Faber, 1971, p. 234: 'Certainty is the end of growth . . . the end of life! And that's the meaning of death to have our understanding flooded with perfect Light!'
23. Thomas Kilroy, *Double Cross*, London: Faber and Faber, 1986, p. 76: 'Identity can be a fiction, Mr. Joyce, and be no less satisfactory on that account'.
24. Thomas Kilroy, *The Seagull by Anton Chekhov: A New Version*, London: Eyre Methuen and the Royal Court Theatre, 1981, p. 14.
25. Thomas Kilroy, 'The O'Neill: A Play', typescript, p, 55.
26. *Ibid.*, p. 76.
27. *Ibid.*, pp. 124-25.
28. *Ibid.*, pp. 125-26.
29. Thomas Kinsella, 'The Irish Writer', in *Davis, Mangan, Ferguson? Tradition & the Irish Writer*, Dublin: Dolmen Press, 1970, p. 66.
30. *Ibid.*, p. 58.
31. Thomas Kilroy, 'The O'Neill', *op. cit.*, p. 125.

32. *Double Cross, op. cit.,* p. 28.
33. Thomas Kilroy, 'Tea and Sex and Shakespear', revised version, 1988, typescript, pp. 21-22.
34. Patrick Kavanagh, 'On Raglan Road', in *Collected Poems,* London: Macgibbon & Kee, 1964, p. 186.
35. Helen Lucy Burke's review for *The Sunday Tribune,* 15 September 1991, was among the most hostile. It obtusely demanded realism where the play tries to transcend realism. See the published text, *The Madame MacAdam Travelling Theatre,* London: Methuen, 1991.
36. Seamus Heaney, *The Cure at Troy: A Version of Sophocles' Philoctetes,* London: Faber and Faber in association with Field Day, 1990, p. 77. The Chorus calls for a marriage between history and hope: 'So hope for a great sea-change/On the far side of revenge'. This speech plainly has reference to the contemporary political situation in Northern Ireland.

JOHN MCGAHERN: A NEW IMAGE?

John Cronin

1. *Nightlines,* London: Faber & Faber, 1970, p. 135.
2. John Montague, *A Chosen Light,* London: McGibbon & Kee, 1967, p. 36.
3. *The Barracks,* and *The Dark,* London; Faber & Faber, 1963 and 1965 respectively.
4. *The Leavetaking,* London: Faber & Faber, 1974.
5. *Amongst Women,* London: Faber & Faber, 1990.
6. *Getting Through,* and *High Ground,* London: Faber & Faber, 1978 and 1985 respectively.
7. Denis Sampson, 'A Conversation with John McGahern', in *Canadian Journal of Irish Studies,* 17, 1, (July 1985), p. 13. Hereinafter referred to as Sampson.
8. James Joyce, *A Portrait of the Artist as a Young Man,* London: Jonathan Cape, 1968, p. 171.
9. Sampson, *ibid.*
10. Patrick Kavanagh, *Collected Poems,* London: McGibbon & Kee, 1964, p. 127.
11. Terence Killeen, 'Versions of Exile: A Reading of *The Leavetaking*', in *Canadian Journal of Irish Studies,* 17, 1, (July 1991), p. 76.
12. Eileen Kennedy, 'Q. & A. with John McGahern', in *Irish Literary Supplement,* 3, 1, (Spring 1984), p. 40.
13. Sampson, p. 16.
14. *Ibid.*
15. *The Leavetaking,* revised version, London: Faber & Faber, 1984.
16. *Ibid.,* Preface.

17. *Ibid.*
18. *The Pornographer*, London: Faber & Faber, 1979.
19. *High Ground*, p. 156.
20. 'The Image', in *Honest Ulsterman* (December 1968), p. 10.
21. 'The Image' (revised), in *Canadian Journal of Irish Studies*, 17, 1, (July 1991), p. 12.
22. *Honest Ulsterman*, p. 10.
23. *Canadian Journal of Irish Studies*, p. 12.
24. *Honest Ulsterman*, p. 10.

IN SEARCH OF THE ROSY GRAIL:
THE CREATIVE PROCESS IN THE NOVELS OF JOHN BANVILLE

Rüdiger Imhof

BANVILLE'S NOVELS:

Birchwood. London: Secker & Warburg, 1973 (referred to in quotations as *B*).
The Book of Evidence. London: Secker & Warburg, 1989 (referred to in quotations as *BE*).
Doctor Copernicus. Secker & Warburg, 1976 (referred to in quotations as *C*).
Kepler. London: Secker & Warburg, 1981 (referred to in quotations as *K*).
Mefisto. London: Secker & Warburg, 1986 (referred to in quotations as *M*).
The Newton Letter. London: Secker & Warburg, 1982 (referred to in quotations as *NL*).
Nightspawn. London: Secker & Warburg, 1971 (referred to in quotations as *N*).

1. Cf. my *John Banville: A Critical Introduction.* Dublin: Wolfhound Press, 1989, p. 71.
2. Actually, Gabriel speaks of 'the fall and rise of Birchwood', thus reverting the historical paradigm and slyly hinting at an inversion of generic conventions pertaining to the Big House novel; cf. Susanne Burgstaller, '"This Lawless House" - John Banville's Post Modernist Treatment of the Big-House Motif', in: O. Rauchbauer (ed.), *Ancestral Voices. The Big House in Anglo-Irish Literature.* Hildesheim, Zurich, New York: George Olms, 1992, p. 244.
3. Cecil Day Lewis, *The Poetic Image.* London: Cape, repr. 1969, p. 68.
4. Rainer Maria Rilke, *Duino Elegies*, trans.. with intro. and commentary by J.B. Leishman & Stephen Spender. London: Chatto & Windus, repr. 1981, p. 85.

5. Cf. the chapter on *The Newton Letter* in my study.
6. Cf. the chapter on *Mefisto* in my study.
7. Martin Gardner, *The Ambidextrous Universe*, Harmondsworth: Penguin, repr. 1982.
8. *A Nietzsche Reader*, selected & translated with an intro. by R.J. Hollingdale. Harmondsworth: Penguin, 1977, p. 83.
9. *Ibid.*, p. 84.
10. Friedrich Nietzsche, *Human, All Too Human*, trans. R.J. Hollingdale with introduction by Erich Heller. Cambridge: CUP, repr. 1988, p. 107.
11. Cf. O'Brien, p. 89.
12. Vladimir Nabokov, *The Annotated Lolita*, ed. with preface, introduction and notes by Alfred Appel, Jr. New York, Toronto: McGraw-Hill, 1970.
13. An unusual combination in that the two fields represent polarities in science, signifying not a means of managing the chaos that Freddie perceives but a confirmation of such.
14. Joe McMinn notes about the painting: 'There is no need to hunt down the painting or its author: I take the picture to be a fiction [. . .]' (McMinn, note 2, p. 134). Maybe there is no need to hunt down the painting or its author, but McMinn is certainly wrong in considering the picture a fiction. As a matter of superfluous interest, the painting has been variously attributed, not to 'Rembrandt and Frans Hals' (*BE*, p. 104), but to Vermeer, de Groot and Valentiner, and it hangs in a museum in Budapest. Its title is 'Portrait of a Lady in Dark Blue' . It is a fact that McMinn, had he researched more fastidiously, should have discovered. Incidentally, Banville himself identified the painting on a books programme broadcast by RTE on the occasion of the publication of *The Book of Evidence* .
15. Joe McMinn is wrong in assuming that the woman in the painting which Freddie steals and later dumps in a ditch, thus putting paid to any notion of cause and effect – a notion he derides -, recalls Anna Behrens. Contrary to McMinn's argument, Freddie's last image of Anna before leaving America is not of her standing beside a window (*BE*, p. 72), rather the last recorded memory before their abrupt departure for Europe is that of Daphne by the window.
16. McMinn notes (pp. 116-18) that Freddie murders a servant, a member of a social stratum beneath his own. His father prided himself on being a 'Castle Catholic' , and of his mother he says that she is a descendant of 'King Billy's henchmen' (*BE*, p. 51). He also mentions 'the burden of birth and education' (*BE*, p. 32) that falls from him in low dives such as Wally's. When he is led away from the police station and notices the infuriated people shaking their fists at him, he realises, 'for the first time, it was *one of theirs* [he] had killed' (BE, p. 211).

17. I wish to acknowledge my indebtedness for this argument and other points to Donal O'Donoghue.
18. 'Stepping into the lime light – and the chaos', *The Irish Times*, 21 October 1989.
19. Rainer Maria Rilke, *The Notebook of Malte Laurids Brigge.* Oxford: OUP, repr. 1984, pp. 19f.

INDEX